Kingston Frontenac Public Library

W9-BUF-092

JUL 2013

GREAT GLUTEN-FREE VEGAN EATS

FROM AROUND THE WORLD

FANTASTIC, ALLERGY-FREE ETHNIC RECIPES

ALLYSON KRAMER

© 2013 Fair Winds Press
Text © 2013 Allyson Kramer
Photography © 2013 Fair Winds Press

First published in the USA in 2013 by
Fair Winds Press, a member of
Quayside Publishing Group
100 Cummings Center
Suite 406-L
Beverly, MA 01915-6101
www.fairwindspress.com

All rights reserved. No part of this book may be reproduced or utilized, in any form or by any means, electronic or mechanical, without prior permission in writing from the publisher.

17 16 15 14 13   1 2 3 4 5

ISBN: 978-1-59233-548-0

Digital edition published in 2013
eISBN: 978-1-61058-746-4

Library of Congress Cataloging-in-Publication Data

Kramer, Allyson.
  Great gluten-free vegan eats from around the world : fantastic, allergy-free ethnic recipes / Allyson Kramer.
     pages cm
  Summary: "Great Gluten-Free Vegan Eats from Around the World is a cookbook for the home chef who likes to explore a world of cuisines, regardless of allergies or dietary restrictions. Step inside and travel the globe while still adhering to your plant-based, gluten-free diet with ethnic entrees you may have thought were off-limits, but are actually even better re-imagined! From European classics like Fig Pastries with Clotted Cream and English Cottage Pie to Caribbean specialties like Jamaican Jerk Tofu and Plantain and Potato Soup, you'll dine on delicious dishes from all around the globe, while still pleasing every palate at your table. —Provided by publisher.
  Includes bibliographical references and index.
  ISBN 978-1-59233-548-0 (hardback) -- ISBN 978-1-61058-746-4 (digital edition)
  1. Gluten-free diet--Recipes. 2. Vegan cooking. 3. International cooking. 4. Food allergy--Diet therapy--Recipes. I. Title.
  RM237.86.K734 2013
  641.5'636--dc23

                                                                          2012045854

Cover and book design by Rita Sowins / Sowins Design
Page layout by Daria Perreault
Photography by Allyson Kramer

Printed and bound in China

The information in this book is for educational purposes only. It is not intended to replace the advice of a physician or medical practitioner. Please see your health care provider before beginning any new health program.

This book is dedicated to my beautiful
friends who reside all over the world.
You constantly inspire me to try out new
foods and enjoy flavors I've never experienced
before, many of which have now become staples
in my own pantry here on the East Coast of
the United States. My kitchen has never smelled
so good thanks to all of you.

CONTENTS

INTRODUCTION

The world is full of mysterious and amazing life that makes up what we call our ecosystem. In that ecosystem exist plants, whose value and contribution to our survival as a species and as individuals may be greater than we will ever know. There are plants that better our eyesight, heal our ailments, and nourish our mind, body, and soul.

AS I STUDY THE EARTH'S COUNTLESS SPECIES of edible plants, I have been astounded to find not only the vast differences, but the incredible similarities among them as they are scattered about the globe. For example, apples, pears, and plums can all be found in the same temperate climate from the midwestern United States to China.

Many fruits may grow in hot climates, but did you know that a relative of the cherimoya, a tropical fruit, grows in the United States? Yep, the rolling hills of West Virginia and surrounding areas are home to a peculiar tree called the pawpaw, which has a custardy, almost banana-like interior and is the only tree of this species found outside of the tropics. All over the world you can find these striking similarities and relatives of plants growing and thriving in different regions—all of them sharing two very important qualities: they taste great and are highly nutritious.

My goal with *Great Gluten-Free Vegan Eats from Around the World* is to introduce you to the amazing food that's featured in different cultures and inspire you to seek out more "exotic" eats as well as embrace other countries' cuisines. No matter where people live in the world, they all love good food. And people from all over the world have done an inspiring job in using the regional fruits and vegetables to their culinary advantage. From moles in Mexico to lolly cakes in New Zealand, we all could stand to gain a little more culture. And why not start where it matters most? Our stomachs!

Even though most chain supermarkets in the United States carry a great many foods from around the world, some of the best places to seek out global delicacies—such as nori wraps, certain spices including asafetida and curry leaves, and gram flour—are Asian, Indian, Mexican, and African markets, if you're fortunate enough to have them nearby. I am a big fan of these kinds of food stores and recommend you become one, too, if you aren't already. They are full of the most tantalizing ingredients you won't find at a typical American chain market. From fresh cactus at your local Mexican grocery to stunning dragon fruit at your neighborhood Asian market, these grocery stores are often a goldmine of culinary delights.

Even though many of these foods may seem strange at first glance, they are really not all too different from many foods included in the Standard American Diet. In fact, many of the world's continental cuisines are heavily influenced by one another. You'd be hard-pressed to find a French dish not romanced with India's vast spices and the Middle East's exotic fruits. And yet the southeastern United States and West Africa share such a similar penchant for comfort food that the cuisines have many staples in common such as peanuts, peppers, rice, sweet potatoes, leafy greens, and beans.

When writing this book, I mapped out all the places from where many common fruits, vegetables, grains, herbs, and spices we use today originated and ended up with a fascinating spiderweb of paths. From trading, importing, and exporting, foods from all over ended up in different parts of the world from travel and conquest, and that's how we get the global cuisines we have today. Many dishes are native or local to the region in which they exist (or were introduced early on) and eventually, through exportation, incorporated more ingredients found in other parts of the world

I have broken down each chapter by continental cuisine, but keep in mind that these recipes originate from many places, including my own region of the world, the midwestern United States. There's a bit of culinary fusion going on where various cuisines overlap, or, in some instances, I just went overboard with inspiration and felt the recipe fit well with the particular continental cuisine. I've tried to match them as closely as possible to the continent or country they derive from or were inspired by utilizing my knowledge of the region's cuisine. I didn't want this to be a book about segregating the many regional cuisines into such different categories, but rather a collection of recipes that are an integration of flavors and a celebration of cultures, ideas, inventions, and tastes … that make the world go 'round.

Chapter 1

GLOBAL INGREDIENT GUIDE

Many ingredients in this book may be unfamiliar to those of us not used to following a vegan and gluten-free diet or even to those of us not skilled at cooking different foods outside of our native cuisines. Once you're familiar with the vast array of fruits, vegetables, grains, beans, herbs, and spices the world has to offer, you'll see how fun they are to integrate into your own cooking. Most of these items are usually pretty easy to get a hold of if you look in the right places. Be sure to read through all these descriptions and become acquainted with the listed foods, as many that I mention are used extensively throughout this book.

AROUND-THE-WORLD INGREDIENTS

Agave

An excellent vegan honey substitute, agave is sweeter than sugar and comes from the same cactus as tequila, which is found in Mexico. I love to use this in dressings and places where I need sweetening but don't want the added heat to make any sugar crystals dissolve. If using in baking, be aware that agave browns quicker than sugar and may send out a false sense of doneness.

Asafetida (asafeotida)

This spice, also known as *hing* in India, is used widely in Indian cooking and imparts a wonderful onion or garlic flavor. Warning: this spice has a very potent and unpleasant odor and must be kept in a sealed jar to prevent it from ruining the tastes and smells of other spices kept close to it. But trust that once the spice cooks, the flavor becomes warming and savory, much like roasted garlic and shallots.

Arugula

This is a lovely small leafy green, often found in mesclun, which has a texture similar to baby spinach and a light, almost peppery, flavor. Also known as rocket, this green has been cultivated for ages and is especially popular in Mediterranean cuisine. It can usually be found next to the spinach and baby greens in your local market. Store in your vegetable crisper for longer-lasting leaves.

Belgian endive

Also known as French endive or witloof, this lettuce yields a very small head with creamy yellow or greenish leaves. Wonderful both cooked and eaten raw, these beautiful, bitter-tasting leaves can usually be found in supermarkets or natural foods stores from late winter to early summer. Most of the world's supply of endive comes from France.

Black salt

This pinkish-colored salt, also known as *kala namak*, is high in sulfur and is used most often in Indian and Pakistani cuisine in conjunction with an abundance of other spices. Black salt is great for adding into many dishes, especially tofu scrambles and similar dishes where an egg flavor is desired. Black salt also goes very well with foods made from chickpea flour and can often be found listed as an ingredient in prepackaged Indian snack foods.

Cardamom

Cardamom is part of the ginger family and grown for its aromatic seeds, which can be green or black. It has a very strong, warm, citrusy flavor. This spice is the third most expensive spice in the world, just behind saffron and vanilla beans. Seed pods can be left whole if they are to be removed after cooking, or the seeds can be ground into a fine powder and incorporated into many dishes from baked goods to curries.

Celeriac

This somewhat unfortunate-looking bulbous root, which grows wild in Northern Europe, is pleasantly celery-like in flavor once the tough outer skin is removed and the tender pale flesh inside is revealed. In fact, it is actually a variety of celery grown not for its crisp and green stalks, but for its white bulbous root. Peel and grate for an exceptional addition to salads or dice into cubes and sauté lightly along with other root veggies, like carrots, parsnips, or potatoes.

Chia seeds

Chia is fast becoming a popular addition to many peoples' diets. Once known in the United States as only part of a gag gift commodity, chia seeds are finally getting the recognition they deserve as a superfood. Chia was coveted as a food source by Aztecs in pre-Columbian times and possibly regarded to be as important as maize. Particularly great as an egg replacer when ground and mixed with water to form a sticky paste, chia is also fantastic incorporated in many other foods such as salads, flavored water, jellies, and smoothies. High in protein and omega-3 and -6 fatty acids, this tiny seed is a great addition to just about anything because it has a very mild flavor and barely perceivable crunch when used whole.

Cilantro

This small-leafed herb is best if purchased fresh, as the flavor of the fresh versus dried is quite different. Some people actually have an aversion to the flavor of fresh cilantro and believe it tastes "soapy," but many folks (such as myself) tend to adore its odorous qualities and crunchy, clean-tasting leaves. Seek out crisp, dark-green leaves for best flavor. It is used widely all over the world, particularly in warmer climates, and is also known as Chinese parsley.

Coconut milk

This is a perfect full-bodied milk for replacing heavy cream and also for ice cream making. Seek out the canned variety, which comes in light and full-fat versions and works similarly to heavy cream. Canned coconut milk is used often in South Indian and Asian cooking.

Another variety of coconut milk comes in a carton, like almond milk, and is much more suitable for drinking than the canned variety. It is thinner, has a milder coconut flavor, and is often located in the refrigerated section of grocery stores.

Coriander

This spice is the seed of the leafy green referred to as cilantro. The taste of the ground seed is similar to fresh cilantro, with an earthier, almost astringent, aftertaste. This spice blends wonderfully with turmeric and is used often in Indian cuisine.

Cumin

Cumin is a spice you will always find in my pantry in both ground and whole seed form. It's so versatile and essential to many great dishes, from chili to stew to curries. Used throughout the world, particularly in Indian and Mexican cuisines, it imparts a thick, almost smoky flavor. You can find both powdered cumin and cumin seeds in most supermarkets' spice sections.

Curry leaves

The fragrant leaves that come from the curry tree are not to be confused with the European invention referred to as curry powder, which is simply a mixture of spices in an attempt to re-create the unique and robust flavor of curry leaves. When simmered in sauces or sautéed with veggies, the leaves impart an irreplaceable flavor that transforms dishes, especially when mixed with other spices such as turmeric, coriander, and cumin. It is available in Indian and African markets.

Dill

This feathery-leafed herb is a relative of parsley and has been used since ancient times as a seasoning. Its fresh leaves, dried leaves (called dill weed), and seeds are used extensively in many various cuisines around the world. In parts of India, it is enjoyed as a vegetable rather than an herb.

Dulse flakes

This is a dried seaweed often available near Asian or vegan cooking ingredients in many supermarkets or natural foods stores and usually sold in a shaker or bag. Sprinkle liberally on foods to add iron, calcium, B vitamins, and the distinct flavor of the sea.

Fennel (bulb)

This delicately licorice-flavored and rough-textured bulbous veggie is from the same plant that produces fennel seeds. It is indigenous to the Mediterranean but has made its way all over the world and into many cuisines. Peel and shave using a mandoline for best texture to add to salads and soups. Chop roughly and add to stir-fries or sauté gently in olive oil.

Fennel seed

Add fennel seeds to a sauté to bring out their robust anise or licorice flavor. Seek out green seeds for the most intense flavor. Fennel works beautifully along with tomatoes and oregano to create a delicious Italian-style seasoning.

Flaxseed

Flaxseed, both whole and in meal form, is located in your supermarket's natural foods section or any natural foods store. Flaxseed does not easily digest or bind when it is whole, but a whirl through your spice grinder makes it perfect for baking and using as a substitute for egg whites in many recipes. Use 1 tablespoon (7 g) flaxseed meal plus 2 tablespoons (28 ml) water to make an egg-like mixture that replaces one egg in many cookies and other baked recipes.

Galangal

Galangal is a rhizome—the stems of certain plants that grow underground—that is related to ginger and shares a similar appearance, but has a very different taste. Galangal has a taste that resembles pepper and is used throughout various parts of Asia, including Thailand and Indonesia. Seek out fresh galangal, generally located next to fresh ginger, from an Asian market or upscale grocery.

Garam masala

This spice, which literally translates to "hot mixture," is actually pungent rather than piquant and is used in many dishes throughout India. Although the exact ingredients in the mixture can vary from one region of India to the next and even one spice jar to the next, a typical garam masala will include toasted peppercorns, cinnamon, cumin, cloves, and cardamom.

Ginger

This fragrant rhizome, which is related to cardamom and turmeric, can be found dried, candied, fresh, and pickled, and all versions are loved around the world for their slightly spicy and unique flavor. Ginger works well in both sweet and savory applications. Used extensively in many types of Asian cooking and even touted as a stomach ailment remedy, gingerroot is easy to locate in most markets, often in the produce section.

Gram flour

Also known as chickpea flour, garbanzo bean flour, or besan, this flour is almost as versatile and lovable as the chickpea itself. Use to make frittatas (see page 71), as a breading for frying, or even as a thickener for stews. This is a flour that I always have on hand. Although you can purchase this flour in small quantities from typical grocery store chains in the natural foods or gluten-free sections, I find it much more economical—not to mention better tasting—to purchase gram flour from Indian groceries or even online in larger quantities.

Habanero peppers

Touted as some of the spiciest, or piquant, peppers in the world, these small, teardrop-shaped beauties add a lot of depth and a good dose of heat to whatever dish they are added to. Retain the seeds and pith for an even bigger burst of heat. Habaneros can burn the skin and or/eyes if handled improperly, so wear food-grade gloves when slicing or de-seeding. If sautéing, keep your face away from the steam produced by the habaneros, as it can irritate your eyes or throat if inhaled.

Hearts of palm

You can find these delicious innards of a coconut palm tree in most grocery stores, either canned or jarred. The texture of these vegetables is somewhere in between artichoke hearts and pickles, and they possess a mild and creamy flavor that mingles well with crisp lettuces or breads.

Jackfruit

This fruit is one of the largest in the world, with a spiky exterior and segmented interior. When green, the flavor of jackfruit is quite mild and admittedly more savory than sweet, with a slightly astringent aftertaste, making it a perfect meat substitute. Once sautéed, the wedges of this fruit turn tender and stringy, not unlike pulled pork. Easiest to locate in canned form, jackfruit is available in many Asian grocery stores as well as online.

Lentils

Lentils have been part of the human diet since Neolithic times and make a solid addition to any pantry because of their versatility and quick cooking time with no need to soak beforehand. Available in many different varieties, black beluga lentils hold up well to applications such as burgers and taco fillings, whereas red lentils work best in soups by dissolving into their own broth.

Lemon verbena

This lemony herb is actually a tree and is used in many medicinal applications and perfumes, as well as a pungent flavoring agent for many foods. It tastes similar to lemon zest and should be cut into a chiffonade to gently garnish foods, or the leaves can be used whole in tea. It is often available in garden centers, and I've had the best luck growing my own small plants of lemon verbena rather than trying to source it at a grocery market. It's a hardy plant and produces well in hot heat or cooler temps.

Lemongrass

This stalky plant, which is a tropical grass, has a magnificently lemony flavor and is used throughout Asian cuisine. Too tough to simply chop up, lemongrass is best used if dried, ground, and frozen or bundled in a cheesecloth (for sauces and soups) and removed once finished cooking.

Kale

Available in a variety of colors and textures, kale is a rising star in the leafy greens world, making appearances in everything from smoothies to kale chips. Eaten raw with a little massaged-in salt and lemon juice as a salad base or chiffonaded and added to sautés, this green makes a great addition to any meal of the day. Kale is not only rich in calcium but also has anti-cancer properties!

Masa harina flour

This flour, which is made from corn specially treated with lime, is the crux of many foods in Mexican cuisine, including tamales and tortillas. This versatile flour can usually be found at many chain supermarkets but is best sourced from a Mexican grocery if you're lucky to have one around. Make sure it is certified gluten free.

Nutritional yeast

This nonactive yeast has a flaky texture and cheesy flavor. Like the name suggests, this nutrient-dense ingredient is high in B vitamins and is a complete protein. It is perfect for giving food a cheesier taste, from dusting on vegetables before roasting to sprinkling on popcorn. It also makes wonderful cheese sauces, when mixed with a nondairy milk.

Okra

Okra is a tall, stalky vegetable that thrives in hot climates and is used extensively in African, Indian, and Southern American cuisine. This plant, valued for its tender and tasty seedpods, is also known as "lady fingers" outside the United States. Choose small pods for best flavor and texture. Larger pods can have an undesirable and sometimes inedible woody texture. If you ever get a chance to grow okra in your own summer garden, do so; its huge, beautiful flowers make for a special treat each time it fruits.

King oyster mushrooms

These mushrooms, related to the smaller mushroom known simply as oyster mushrooms, are large and have a neutral taste when raw. Cooked, the texture becomes reminiscent of sea scallops, as seen in the Seared "Scallops" with White Truffle Sauce (see page 190).

Parsnips

This root veggie looks just like a pale carrot and has a similar texture, with a bit sharper, yet sweeter, taste than a carrot. Use it as you would carrots by roasting, shredding, boiling, braising, and puréeing. It is one of the closest relatives of parsley, which can also be bred to develop a root similar to a parsnip.

Pepitas

Pepitas are small, green pumpkin seeds with the hull removed that are used extensively in Mexican and some South American cuisine. They are excellent additions to salads and are wonderfully flavorful much like sunflower seeds.

Quinoa

Quinoa is a wonderful gluten-free grain that originates in South America—where it was once secondary only to the potato in importance as a food staple—and is touted for its extensive nutritional profile. High in protein, fiber, and iron, quinoa is a great alternative to rice and other grains in everyday applications.

Red bean paste (anko)

Anko is the Japanese term for red bean paste, which is also known as *ogura*. Japan is not the only country that enjoys this sweet confection generally used as a filling. Korea and China also incorporate this ingredient into many of their dishes. The paste is prepared by cooking and mashing adzuki beans and then sweetening the mashed beans with sugar. This paste is easy to source in most Asian markets and is available either "mashed" or "smooth," although the smooth variety is typically only used as a filling in Chinese pastries.

Serrano peppers

These gorgeous peppers are similar to jalapeños, but they have a touch sweeter flavor and are more piquant. Originating in Mexico, these peppers are used throughout Mexican cuisine and are oftentimes eaten raw.

Shallots

Originating in Asia and popular in European cuisine, this little reddish bulb is similar in taste to the common onion, but much mellower in flavor and often quite striking in color if used raw. I use shallots often in cooking where red onions or white onions may impart too harsh of a flavor.

Sorrel

This somewhat elusive herb is leafy and similar to spinach in texture and flavor, but often difficult to find at grocery stores. A common ingredient in the Greek dish spanakopita, sorrel is also often added to salads and used similarly to spinach both fresh and cooked. Sorrel contains a toxic substance that gives it its fruity taste, and if used in high amounts (way more than ever called for in most recipes), the plant can be fatal. Oftentimes hard to spot alongside regular herbs, specialty stores or farmers' markets will carry sorrel in very small quantities. If you can't find sorrel, use spinach as a substitute.

Soy curls

Butler Soy Curls are a great meat alternative to have around, as they pick up virtually any flavor and have an uncanny texture that's similar to cooked chicken.

If you're lucky enough to live in Portland, Oregon, you can find Soy Curls from local Food Fight grocers; otherwise, see the Grocery Guide (page 202) for a list of retailers that carry it.

Soyrizo

This vegetable-based meat alternative tastes and looks strikingly like chorizo. Use crumbled up in a variety of recipes or as a base in burgers—mixed with cooked lentils is fantastic—or in stews. Generally sold in the refrigerated section of many grocery stores, Trader Joe's brand is one variety that I enjoy cooking with. I also have a recipe for homemade Soyrizo (see recipe, page 103).

Superfine brown rice flour

This flour is growing wildly in popularity simply because it's one of the best gluten-free flours available today. Authentic Foods' brand is the main producer of this flour, which is made from the brown rice grain, just as regular brown rice flour is made, except that it is double milled—resulting in a finer and much silkier texture than regular-grind brown rice flour. When used in baking it produces a lighter, airier recipe, similar to that of glutinous flour. Don't try and replicate the recipes that call for superfine brown rice flour with regular or coarser-ground brown rice flour, as the results will be grainier and unpredictable.

Swiss chard

Fun Fact: The name "Swiss chard" was developed by sellers of catalog-order seeds in the 1800s to distinguish this broad leafy green from the French variety of spinach. This large and nutritious leafy green vegetable is very versatile and often used in Mediterranean cooking as well as cuisines from all over the world. A relative to the beetroot, chard has crisp, water-packed stalks, often seen in a variety of colors (called rainbow chard).

Tarragon

Although a few varieties exist, French tarragon is the one most called for in recipes. This leafy herb has a fennel-like flavor and is used extensively in French cooking. Described as one of the *herbes fines* in French cuisine, along with parsley, chives, and chervil, it should be added at the end of making a dish because the leaves are delicate and the flavor can easily be overwhelmed by other flavors in a recipe and completely lost to long cooking times, unlike heartier herbs such as oregano or bay leaf.

Tempeh

This fermented soy food, which originates from Indonesia, is often used as a meat replacement in vegan cuisine. Available in natural foods stores or suppliers of Indonesian groceries, the texture is much drier than tofu, and often it has a much more potent flavor. Tempeh should be slightly marbled in color and have little to no fragrance when fresh.

TVP (textured vegetable protein)

This is a meat analogue made from soy protein or soy flour. It is a versatile meat substitute that stores for up to one year if kept dried and when rehydrated resembles ground beef. It has practically no flavor, which makes it great for absorbing flavors from the marinade in which it is rehydrated. You can find TVP in natural food stores as well as many chain supermarkets. I recommend purchasing Bob's Red Mill brand as it is guaranteed gluten-free, whereas some of the other brands may contain wheat as a filler ingredient.

Tomatillo

These small green tomato-shaped fruits are a member of the nightshade family and are a main ingredient in Mexican cuisine. They are best when cooked lightly to release their flavor, but also tasty when used raw in salsas. Tomatillos have a lot of pectin and will thicken sauces if simmered, cooled, and then chilled.

Turmeric

Turmeric is related to ginger and galangal as a rhizome and originated in India or Southeast Asia. Although you can find it fresh at Indian or Asian markets, dried turmeric is almost always used. Use turmeric alone for a distinct flavor similar to saffron and a very telling yellow color that easily stains hands.

Watercress

This is a leafy and, like its name implies, aquatic, veggie that is often used on sandwiches and salads. Known as one of the oldest harvested greens, it has a little cluster of round leaves and hollow stems and can be enjoyed in a variety of ways. Located in your produce section, generally by the arugula or kale, watercress has an almost succulent texture, with a crisp clean finish reminiscent of both celeriac and baby spinach with peppery undertones.

Yam

Often confused with but completely unrelated to sweet potatoes, yams are tuberous vines that originated in both Africa and Asia. Although their taste and texture is similar, yams have a thicker skin and generally a starchier texture than sweet potatoes.

Chapter 2

EXPLORING AFRICAN CUISINE

Africa is home to a wide variety of cuisines that both originated from the continent and were introduced by other countries. The northern part of Africa is where many of our favorite foods originate, as well as some of the oldest cultivated foods on Earth. The center of this foodie gold mine is pretty much where Egypt is today, referred to as the Fertile Crescent. Basic staples, as well as a variety of foods considered delicacies, came from this region more than 4,000 years ago, including olives, wine, chickpeas, wheat, and lentils. Northern Africa is home to mankind's earliest agricultural efforts and continues to be a treasured area for its fertile soil and great climate.

Because Africa is so large, the cuisines tend to differ depending on the region. West African cuisine is fairly heavy in meat and spices, whereas in Central Africa, little meat or dairy is consumed because it is difficult to come by. One major crop that is featured prominently throughout the continent is groundnuts, or peanuts, as they are known in the United States, and I made sure to include plenty of recipes that contain this beloved, plant-based protein.

CREAMY DREAMY KALAMATA HUMMUS

To make the creamiest hummus ever, be sure your chickpeas are dried (not canned), soaked overnight, slightly overcooked, and peeled. Also, cool your chickpeas completely before blending. Trust me, it's worth the extra bit of effort.

• • • • • • • • • • • • • • • • YIELD: 3 CUPS (738 G.) HUMMUS • • • • • • • • • • • • • • • •

3 cups (600 g) dried chickpeas

½ cup (120 ml) Kalamata olive juice

2 tablespoons (30 g) tahini

¼ cup (60 ml) water

Zest and juice of 1 lime

Dash fine sea salt

1 cup (380 g) minced Kalamata olives

To easily cook the chickpeas, soak the dried chickpeas in water at least 6 hours and up to overnight. Place the chickpeas in a large stockpot, cover with water at least 5 inches (13 cm) above the chickpeas, and bring to a boil. Reduce the heat to a constant simmer and cook about 2 hours or until very tender. Rinse under cold water and rub between your hands to remove the thin skins or place the cooked chickpeas in a large bowl of cold water. As you rub and remove the skins, you can easily skim the water to remove them. Let cool completely before proceeding with the hummus.

Combine the cooked chickpeas, olive juice, tahini, water, lime zest and juice, and sea salt in a food processor and run until very smooth, at least 7 minutes. Fold in the Kalamata olives and blend until the Kalamatas become chopped evenly. Chill for 2 hours before serving.

For a fun presentation, serve with red cabbage wedges and eat as you would tortilla chips.

Olive Trivia

Kalamata olives have deep, rich, eggplant-colored flesh and come from the Kalamata region of Greece. Unlike other varieties, Kalamatas cannot be harvested while still green and have to be handpicked because of their fragile nature. This makes them somewhat of a delicacy compared to common black or green olives.

SEASIDE AVOCADO DIP

This recipe is modeled after a dip from Madagascar that is similar to guacamole but includes anchovies as a main ingredient. Marinated mushrooms and dulse flakes work together in this recipe to add a hint of the sea.

• YIELD: 3 CUPS (780 G) DIP • • • • • • • • • • • • • • • • • • •

FOR THE MARINATED MUSHROOMS:

- 1½ cups (105 g) sliced button mushrooms
- 3 tablespoons (9 g) dulse flakes
- 5 to 10 dashes liquid smoke
- 1 tablespoon (15 ml) olive oil
- 1½ teaspoons fine sea salt
- ½ tablespoon vegan Worcestershire sauce
- ⅔ cup (160 ml) water

FOR THE REST OF THE DIP:

- 4 ripe avocados, peeled and pitted
- 1½ tablespoons (23 ml) lime juice
- 1 teaspoon lime zest
- 1 tablespoon (15 ml) white wine
- Fine sea salt to taste
- ¼ cup (40 g) minced red onion or shallots

TO MAKE THE MARINATED MUSHROOMS: Plan to marinate the mushrooms at least 2 hours before making the dip. Place the sliced mushrooms in a small bowl and toss with all the other ingredients until well coated. Cover and let rest 1 to 2 hours and up to 4 hours.

Squeeze all the liquid from the mushrooms until they are fairly dry. Chop into ½-inch (1 cm) pieces.

TO MAKE THE DIP: In medium-size bowl, smash the avocados until they are smooth and then stir in the lime juice, lime zest, white wine, and sea salt to taste. Fold in the minced red onions and marinated mushrooms. Serve with your favorite gluten-free crackers.

RECIPE NOTE

If you're not very fond of the flavor of seaweed, leave the dulse flakes out of this recipe and just marinate the mushrooms in the rest of the ingredients.

PEPPERY BANANA, AVOCADO, AND PAPAYA SALAD

This fruity salad's dressing acquires a peppery taste from ground-up papaya seeds used similarly to peppercorns. The seeds not only carry a flavorful bite, they also add a nutritional bonus as they are high in calcium, magnesium, and phosphorous.

· · · · · · · · · · · · · · · · YIELD: 4 MEDIUM-SIZE SALADS · · · · · · · · · · · · · · · ·

FOR THE DRESSING:

½ **ripe banana**

3 **tablespoons (27 g) papaya seeds**

5 **tablespoons (75 ml) lime juice**

2 **heaping teaspoons grated ginger**

1 **tablespoon (20 g) agave**

1 **small carrot, shredded**

1 **tablespoon (15 ml) extra-virgin olive oil (optional)**

Dash nutmeg

¼ **teaspoon sea salt**

FOR THE SALAD:

5 **cups (150 g) fresh baby spinach leaves**

1½ **bananas, thinly sliced**

½ **large papaya, very thinly sliced into strips**

1 **avocado, sliced**

1 **carrot, grated**

Make the dressing by pulsing all the ingredients in a food processor until very smooth and the papaya seeds turn into black flecks.

Toss the baby spinach leaves with the dressing to coat and then divide among 4 salad plates. Top with banana, papaya, avocado, and grated carrot. Serve immediately. Be sure to get a little bit of everything into each bite.

JUST RIPE!

It's easy to tell when a papaya is ripe: The fruit will be soft to the touch, and the skin will have an amber hue.

KALE AND SWISS CHARD SALAD WITH TOASTED PEPITAS

This bright and zesty salad features some of Africa's most prominent foods, such as coconut, lemon, ginger, and dark leafy greens. The combination of ingredients makes for a tangy and tasty side inspired by the brilliant offerings of this continent's cuisine.

• • • • • • • • • • • • • • • • • YIELD: 2 LARGE SALADS OR 4 SMALL SALADS • • • • • • • • • • • • • •

5 leaves kale, any variety

5 leaves Swiss chard, any variety

1 tablespoon (15 ml) lemon juice

½ teaspoon sea salt

1 handful baby spinach

1 carrot, shredded

½ cup (40 g) shredded coconut

2 tablespoons (28 ml) orange juice

1 teaspoon agave, brown rice syrup, or granulated sugar

½ teaspoon grated ginger

½ cup (70 g) toasted pepitas (pumpkin seeds), toasting instructions below

Rinse the kale and chard leaves well and then pat dry with clean kitchen towel. Remove the stems from the leaves and stack the leaves snugly on top of one another and then roll into a cigar shape. Slice across with short cuts to chiffonade the greens. Toss the greens into a bowl along with the lemon juice and sea salt and massage using clean hands until softened, about 5 minutes. Gently toss the massaged kale with the spinach, carrot, and coconut to mix throughout.

In small bowl, stir together the orange juice, agave, and ginger. Drizzle the dressing onto greens and toss to coat. Top with the pepitas before serving.

RECIPE NOTE

To toast the pepitas, spread the seeds onto a very lightly greased baking sheet in a single even layer. Bake in a preheated oven at 375°F (190°C, gas mark 5) until fragrant and golden, about 7 to 10 minutes.

FIERY GINGERED YAM SALAD

This salad is inspired by two of Africa's most often-used crops: ginger and yams. The ginger in this recipe dominates and adds a bit of heat to the salad. Cut it slightly if you'd prefer a less fiery dish.

• YIELD: 4 SMALL SALADS •

3 medium-size white yams

FOR THE DRESSING:

2 cloves garlic, minced

2 tablespoons (16 g) fresh grated ginger

I tablespoon (20 g) agave

½ teaspoon sea salt

Dash nutmeg

⅓ cup (5 g) finely chopped cilantro

I tablespoon (15 ml) lemon juice

I tablespoon (15 ml) coconut milk

8 finely chopped sun-dried tomatoes, soaked in water at least I hour and drained

Preheat the oven to 350°F (180°C, gas mark 4), place the yams on a baking sheet, and loosely cover with aluminum foil. Bake for 1 to 1½ hours or until soft when pierced with a fork. Remove from the oven and let cool briefly until cool enough to handle. Remove the skins and cut into bite-size cubes. Place in a large bowl.

Make the dressing by mixing all the ingredients, except the sun-dried tomatoes, together in a small bowl. Add the sun-dried tomatoes and then drizzle the dressing onto the cooked yams. Toss lightly to coat.

VITA-YAM!

Yams, while being a good source of fiber, also provide a hefty boost of potassium, vitamin B6, vitamin C, and manganese.

ROASTED EGGPLANT AND TOMATO SALAD

This easy side is bursting with umami flavor—a pleasingly subtle,
yet savory taste imparted by glutamate—from the roasted tomatoes and eggplant.
Corn gives it an added sweetness and fresh dill lends a slightly bitter
accent, making this dish quite a treat for one's taste buds.

•••••••••••••••••••••••• YIELD: 3 CUPS (350 G) SALAD ••••••••••••••••••••••••

**1 medium-size thin-skinned
eggplant, cut into 1-inch (2.5 cm)
pieces**

Salt, to taste

**3 cups (450 g) assorted small
tomatoes (cherry, globe, etc.)**

Drizzle olive oil

½ tablespoon ground cumin

1 cup (165 g) cooked corn kernels

2 tablespoons minced (8 g) fresh dill

Preheat the oven to 400°F (200°C, gas mark 6) and line a baking sheet with parchment paper or a silicone mat.

In a medium-size bowl, salt the eggplant gently and then toss with the tomatoes and drizzle with olive oil. Spread the eggplant and the tomatoes onto the prepared baking sheet and roast for about 20 minutes or until the eggplants are golden and the tomatoes are sunken and shiny. Sprinkle the veggies with the cumin.

Toss into a medium-size bowl along with the corn and dill and serve warm or cold. This tastes wonderful on top of tiny toasts made from Pain Ordinaire recipe, (page 51).

DID YOU KNOW?

Eggplant, like the tomato, is a nightshade, making them close relatives; although eggplant is actually botanically classified as a berry.

PEANUTTY PARSNIP AND CARROT SOUP

This delicious and simple soup utilizes one of Africa's most important foods, the groundnut, or peanut, as we commonly refer to it in some parts of the world. The sweetness of parsnip and carrot accent the earthy peanut flavor in this soup quite nicely.

YIELD: 6 SERVINGS

1 bulb garlic, about 7 cloves

5 medium-size carrots, peeled

5 medium-size parsnips, peeled

½ teaspoon olive oil

1 teaspoon sea salt

¼ cup (65 g) peanut butter

1 teaspoon curry powder

4 cups (950 ml) salted vegetable broth

Fine sea salt to taste

Preheat the oven to 400°F (200°C, gas mark 6) to roast the garlic.

Peel off the thick outer skin of the garlic bulb and using a small knife, trim about ½ inch (1 cm) off the pointy end of the bulb to expose the individual cloves, leaving the bottom part completely intact. Place the bulb in the center of an 8 x 8-inch (20 x 20 cm) square of aluminum foil and lightly drizzle with olive oil. Create a loose pouch around the foil and seal. Place the foil pouch on a baking sheet and bake until the cloves are softened and very fragrant, about 40 minutes. Set aside.

Slice the carrots and parsnips into ½-inch (1 cm) wide ovals. Place in a medium-size bowl and toss with olive oil. Spread evenly onto an ungreased baking sheet and salt lightly with about 1 teaspoon of sea salt. Roast for 25 minutes or until the carrots and parsnips are tender and browned on the edges. Let the roasted vegetables cool briefly.

Transfer to a food processor and combine with the roasted garlic, peanut butter, curry powder, and about 1 cup (235 ml) vegetable broth. Process the mixture until it is very smooth, about 5 minutes. Transfer into a pot, add the remaining vegetable broth, and simmer until hot.

Nutty Fact

Did you know that the peanut is not actually a nut at all but a legume that develops underground? The plant's flower starts above ground, but eventually the stalk bends and keeps growing, so that it buries itself underground, where the fruit, or "groundnut," is formed within a pod, known as the shell.

CRISPY CRUNCHY BASMATI RICE FRITTERS

I absolutely adore the surprising texture and ease of this recipe;
they taste a lot like hash browns but contain no potatoes. Although the
recipe involves deep-frying, it makes a great treat for every once in a while.
The extra-crispy outside contrasts with the tender center.
This fritter is a perfect dish to share with company.

•   YIELD: 14 FRITTERS   •

2 tablespoons (14 g) flaxseed meal
¼ cup (60 ml) water
2 cups (370 g) cooked basmati rice
½ cup (68 g) sorghum flour
¼ cup (30 g) tapioca starch
1½ teaspoons sea salt
¼ cup (40 g) grated onion
Scant ½ cup (120 ml) coconut milk
Vegetable oil for frying
Black pepper to taste
Paprika to taste

Preheat a deep fryer to 360°F (182°C).

Combine the flaxseed meal with the water in a small bowl and allow the mixture to rest until thick, about 5 minutes. In a large bowl, combine the prepared flaxseed meal with the rice, sorghum flour, tapioca starch, sea salt, onion, and coconut milk. Stir until a thick, clumpy dough is formed.

Make into rounded patties, about 1-inch (2.5 cm) thick and carefully place into the hot oil. Cook for about 5 minutes or until golden brown. Remove from the oil and place on an absorbent towel. Sprinkle with a generous amount of black pepper and paprika before serving.

RECIPE NOTE

Another variety of these fritters, called *calas*, used to be commonly sold in New Orleans, when people of African descent would make them and sell them on the streets. They were sweet and often served with syrup or finely ground sugar. These basmati fritters, however, are savory and especially great served with spicy Dijon mustard mixed with a touch of vegan mayo and a splash of lemon juice.

MILD OKRA CURRY WITH FRAGRANT YELLOW RICE

Curry leaves, completely unrelated to curry powder, can be sourced
from your local Indian, African, or Asian market or even online.
You definitely don't want to leave them out of this recipe.
They will transform you instantly to Africa with their intensely
inviting and highly unique fragrance. If you happen to come across
curry leaves, buy up a bunch! They freeze beautifully.

· YIELD: 4 SERVINGS ·

FOR THE CURRY:

1 onion, chopped

4 cloves garlic, minced

10 curry leaves, or 1 sprig

2 tablespoons (28 g) coconut oil

1 teaspoon cumin seed

¼ teaspoon cardamom

½ teaspoon coriander

**1 teaspoon white pepper,
adjust to taste**

½ teaspoon ground fennel seeds

¼ teaspoon ground cloves

1 teaspoon fine sea salt

**5 ounces (150 g, about 20 heads)
fresh, not frozen, okra**

2 cups (475 ml) coconut milk

1 tablespoon (4 g) sorghum flour

FOR THE YELLOW RICE:

**1½ cups (278 g) basmati or
jasmine rice**

10 threads saffron

TO MAKE THE CURRY: Sauté the onion, garlic, and curry leaves in the coconut oil over medium-high heat for about 2 minutes. Toss in the spices (through cloves) and stir to coat evenly. Sprinkle with sea salt and cook over medium-high heat, stirring often, until the onions are translucent, about 7 minutes.

Add the okra and sauté an additional 10 to 15 minutes or until the okra pods become tender. Add the coconut milk and cook about 10 more minutes, stirring occasionally to prevent it from sticking.

Add the sorghum flour and cook about 2 more minutes, just to thicken. Remove the curry leaves. Serve over the yellow rice.

TO MAKE THE RICE: Simply cook the rice according to package directions, adding 10 threads of saffron to the water. My favorite method of cooking rice is starting with cold water, adding rice, bringing the water to a rolling boil, and then reducing the heat to low. Let cook, covered, until all water has been absorbed, about 20 minutes for basmati or 25 to 30 minutes for jasmine.

RECIPE NOTE

Okra is best when harvested small; look for bright green, smooth pods, about 2 to 3 inches (5 to 7.5 cm) in length, for best flavor and more importantly, better texture. Large okra pods are very fibrous and difficult to eat!

EASY ONE-POT (JOLLOF) RICE WITH CINNAMON AND CURRY

This recipe is an easy way to get a complex and satisfying dinner on the table quickly, with very little mess because it uses only one pot. This dish is a classic in African cuisine and can be switched up to include a variety of vegetables and spices to suit your liking.

YIELD: 6 servings

- 1 tablespoon (14 g) coconut oil
- 2 tomatoes, blanched, peeled, and chopped
- 2 carrots, sliced into coins
- 1 red onion, diced
- 3 large leaves kale, cut into fine chiffonade
- 1 red pepper, chopped
- 1 teaspoon grated ginger
- 1½ cups (278 g) uncooked basmati rice
- 3 cups (700 ml) salted vegetable broth
- 2 tablespoons (32 g) tomato paste
- 2 bay leaves
- ½ teaspoon nutmeg
- 9 curry leaves
- 1 cinnamon stick
- 1 teaspoon cumin
- ½ to 1 teaspoon red chile flakes
- Sea salt to taste, if desired

In a deep 2-quart (2 L) saucepan with a lid, heat the coconut oil over medium-high heat and then sauté the tomatoes, carrots, onion, kale, red pepper, and ginger until tender, about 5 to 7 minutes. Salt the vegetables lightly while they are cooking.

Once the vegetables are soft, add the rice, vegetable broth, and tomato paste. Toss in the bay leaves, nutmeg, curry leaves, cinnamon stick, cumin, and chile flakes and stir well to combine. Bring to a full boil over high heat. Immediately after the mixture begins to boil, reduce the heat to a simmer and cover with a lid. Check the rice after about 15 minutes, and cook until all liquid has been absorbed, about 20 minutes. Fluff with a fork, remove bay and curry leaves, cinnamon stick, and salt lightly to taste.

RECIPE NOTE

Although this may seem like a perfect quick meal for a night in with the family, in many parts of West Africa, Jollof rice is considered a potluck or party dish. It makes perfect sense, as it's colorful, fragrant, easy to make, and can be transported in the same pot it was cooked in! Not to mention, it's quite a crowd pleaser in the taste department!

SWEET COCONUT ORANGE COOKIES

These cookies resemble macaroons but also have the lovely addition of almond flavor, which adds a touch of sweetness and a lovely bite to the classic cookie.

•••••• YIELD: 12 COOKIES ••••••

2 cups (160 g) sweetened shredded coconut
1 cup (112 g) almond flour
½ cup (115 g) packed dark brown sugar
¼ cup (60 ml) nondairy milk
1 tablespoon (6 g) orange zest

Preheat your oven to 350°F (180°C, gas mark 4). Line a standard-size cookie sheet with parchment paper or a silicone mat. In a large bowl, stir together the coconut, almond flour, brown sugar, nondairy milk, and orange zest until it comes together into a thick dough. You may need to add a tablespoon (15 ml) or more extra nondairy milk to form the dough, but don't add too much. At first it will seem crumbly, but the more you stir, the quicker it comes together.

Divide the dough into 12 cookies and place on the prepared cookie sheet. Bake for 20 to 25 minutes or until lightly golden brown on the edges.

Let the cookies cool completely before serving.

SPICED LENTIL HARIRA

This soup comes together easily and makes a wonderfully fragrant addition to any meal. For a light but satisfying dinner, serve with the Roasted Eggplant and Tomato Salad (page 29).

•••••• YIELD: 6 SERVINGS ••••••

1 large can (28 ounces [785 g]) crushed tomatoes
1 cup (192 g) dried lentils
1 onion, diced
2 stalks celery, sliced
6 cups (1.4 L) salted vegetable broth
1 teaspoon red pepper flakes (more or less depending on your spice tastes)
1 teaspoon coriander powder
½ teaspoon turmeric powder
1 teaspoon cinnamon
½ teaspoon dried ginger
2 cups (480 g) cooked chickpeas (added after cooking soup halfway)
2 tablespoons (15 g) gram flour mixed with ¼ cup (60 ml) water until smooth
½ cup (30 g) chopped parsley
¼ cup (4 g) chopped cilantro
1 teaspoon sea salt, or to taste
2 large lemons, sliced into wedges, for serving

Place all the ingredients through ginger in a large stockpot and bring to a boil over high heat. Reduce the heat to medium, to maintain a constant simmer, and let cook for about 30 minutes or until the lentils are tender. Stir in the chickpeas, gram flour mixture, parsley, and cilantro. Cook an additional 10 minutes to cook the gram flour completely and to thicken the soup. Salt to taste and serve with a lemon wedge.

GAZELLE HORNS (KAAB EL GHAZAL)

The intoxicating flavor of almond dominates these filled cookies. Use plastic wrap to help roll the dough as thin as possible without tearing and cut off any excess dough from the tips once they have been rolled up or else you'll have an uneven dough-to-filling ratio. You're not going to want to miss out on this cookie's almondy ambrosia, so don't let the dough become too thick.

YIELD: 12 COOKIES

1 cup (160 g) superfine brown rice flour

½ cup (85 g) potato starch

½ cup (65 g) sorghum flour

¼ cup (39 g) sweet white rice flour

2 teaspoons xanthan gum

¼ cup (50 g) sugar

7 tablespoons (98 g) vegan margarine

½ cup (120 ml) ice-cold water

1 to 2 additional tablespoons (10 to 20 g) superfine brown rice flour for kneading

4 ounces (115 g) almond paste (make sure it's gluten free, such as Solo brand)

⅓ cup (48 g) white sesame seeds

Preheat your oven to 400°F (200°C, gas mark 6). In a large bowl, whisk together the superfine brown rice flour, potato starch, sorghum flour, sweet white rice flour, xanthan gum, and sugar until well combined. Cut in the margarine using a pastry blender until evenly mixed into the dry ingredients. Form a well in the center of the flours and stir in the ice-cold water using a fork until a tacky dough is formed. Sprinkle the dough lightly with an additional 1 tablespoon (10 g) superfine brown rice flour and knead until soft and pliable. Chill briefly in the refrigerator.

Roll out the dough quite thin between 2 sheets of plastic wrap. Cut out a 4-inch (10 cm) square and place a small rounded cylinder of almond paste in the middle. Roll the dough up around the almond paste like a cigar and gently coax the dough into a half-moon shape to mold around the filling. This takes a bit of practice to get perfect, so don't worry if yours look a little ragged around the edges the first time—they will still taste good! Seal the dough using your fingertips. Place the sesame seeds in a small bowl and press the tops of the rolled cookies into the seeds.

Place the cookies on an ungreased cookie sheet, about 1 inch (2.5 cm) apart, and bake for 25 minutes or until the cookies are golden around the edges and your kitchen is filled with the intoxicating aroma of almonds.

Let cool completely before serving.

RECIPE NOTE

In traditional Moroccan style, these cookies are served with orange flower water for dipping. If you can locate this item in a grocery that carries Moroccan foods, I'd definitely recommend trying it out. The addition of it elevates this recipe to a heavenly level.

BAMBARA PEANUT BUTTER RICE PUDDING

This easy and oh-so-peanutty dessert is a great way to use up any extra basmati rice you may have in your fridge. This porridge is a favorite for Central Africans, where they prepare it similarly using rice, peanut butter, and sugar.

•   YIELD: 4 SERVINGS   •

2 cups (316 g) cooked jasmine rice, cold

¼ cup (60 ml) coconut milk

¼ cup (80 ml) agave or brown rice syrup

1 teaspoon fine sea salt

½ cup (130 g) creamy natural peanut butter

Additional agave for drizzling

1 cup (145 g) crushed peanuts

Cinnamon for topping

In small saucepan over medium-low heat, combine the rice, coconut milk, agave, sea salt, and peanut butter and heat until warm and creamy. Garnish with a drizzle of agave or brown rice syrup and top with crushed peanuts and cinnamon.

RECIPE NOTE

This dessert tastes exceptionally great with add-ins! Try stirring in a few semisweet chocolate chips, small bits of Medjool dates, and a little maple syrup for a super-indulgent treat!

CRUNCHY COCONUT PEANUT CANDY

Adapted from a recipe that caught my attention on the University of Pennsylvania's website, this candy is similar to a brittle peanut butter fudge. It's a quick and delicious treat to whip up because the sugar in the recipe only needs to cook a few minutes, much less than the long cooking times of other homemade candies.

. . . . YIELD: 20 PIECES OF CANDY . . . .

2⅓ cups (467 g) granulated sugar
¼ cup (60 ml) coconut milk
1 cup (85 g) shredded unsweetened coconut
1½ cups (218 g) crushed peanuts

Prepare an 8-inch (20 x 20 cm) baking pan by lining it with parchment paper. Set it aside but keep it close to your cooking area so it will be handy as soon as the candy is fully cooked.

In a 2-quart (2 L) saucepan, over medium heat, warm up the sugar and coconut milk and continue to cook, stirring constantly, until the sugar has turned into a liquid, about 2 minutes. The sugar will still be grainy, but it should be able to flow.

Remove from heat and stir in the coconut and peanuts until well mixed and quickly transfer to the prepared pan. Press down firmly with a fork, or clean hands, to pack the sugar mixture into the mold. The mixture will be loose and crumbly at this time, but if well packed, it will come together nicely when cooled.

Let rest at least 1 hour until completely cooled. Invert the pan to remove the candy and then carefully cut into bite-size pieces. Store in an airtight container for up to 1 week.

SHAPE IT UP!

This candy can also be placed into flexible silicon molds while hot, which will allow you to skip the step of slicing the candy and ensure even shapes every time! Ice cube trays also work well for this, so be creative!

chapter 3

EUROPEAN EATS- BON APPÉTIT!

Europe is home to some of the most coveted cuisines on the planet, including the widely popular dishes of France and Italy. From the exciting tapas of Spain to the comforting meals of Poland and Germany, Europe's diverse contribution to the food world is quite vast and covers a variety of tastes and textures.

As I mentioned in the introduction, many of the dishes we have come to associate with Europe would not exist if it weren't for the contributions of other countries. For instance, olives were brought from Egypt, grapes and figs from the Middle East, and a variety of spices from India. Greece, where foods such as lentils, cabbage, and mustard originated, may be the exception, but the rest of Europe relied heavily on importing many components to create rich and fragrant fare. Eventually Europe began cultivating its own crops and came to create the many food combinations and classic dishes we know and love today.

BLACK OLIVE AND SUN-DRIED TOMATO TAPENADE

A delicious starter to any meal when served with crisp vegetables or small bites of bread, this tapenade features some of the finest flavors in European cuisine. Use as a mix-in to stews and pasta dishes for a ton of added flavor with very little effort.

• YIELD: 1½ CUPS (203 G) TAPENADE • • • • • • • • • • • • • • • • • •

15 sun-dried tomatoes

½ cup (120 ml) water (substitute 3 tablespoons [45 ml] of water with white wine for an extra bit of zing)

1 tablespoon (15 ml) olive oil

1 small red onion, diced

1 clove garlic, sliced

1 teaspoon sea salt, divided

1½ cups (255 g) black olives

In a small bowl, soak the sun-dried tomatoes in the water for about 1 hour or until softened.

While the tomatoes are soaking, heat the olive oil in a medium-size frying pan. Add the onion, garlic, and ½ teaspoon of salt and sauté over medium-high heat until the onions are evenly browned and translucent, about 10 minutes.

Once the tomatoes have soaked, drain well and combine with the sautéed onions and black olives in a food processor. Add the additional sea salt and pulse until all ingredients are combined and the olives and tomatoes are very finely chopped.

Serve on top of flatbreads or gluten-free crackers with a garnish of fresh cilantro.

DID YOU KNOW?

Olive trees are known to have very hardy root systems that can regenerate growth even if the aboveground, or visible, section of the tree is completely destroyed. This means olive trees can have a long lifespan, with some trees confirmed as more than 2,000 years old by way of tree ring analysis and radiocarbon dating.

PAIN ORDINAIRE

This crusty and toothsome white bread is great for serving fresh. It's also perfect for small bites such as mini cucumber tea sandwiches. To make, use a vegetable peeler to slice very thin strips of cucumber and spread slices of toasted bread with vegan mayonnaise. Top with cucumber slices, a dash of salt, and a sprinkle of black pepper and you have yourself a sophisticated and delicious treat to serve with tea.

YIELD: 1 LOAF

- 2½ cups (400 g) superfine brown rice flour
- ½ cup (65 g) cornstarch
- 1 tablespoon (18 g) psyllium husk powder
- 1½ teaspoons baking powder
- 1 teaspoon sea salt
- 2½ packets (20 g) dry active yeast
- ¼ cup (50 g) organic sugar
- 1 cup (235 ml) warm water
- 2 cups (475 ml) warm almond milk, divided
- ½ cup (120 ml) water
- 2 teaspoons vinegar
- ¼ cup (60 ml) + 2 tablespoons (28 ml) olive oil
- 1 tablespoon (12 g) ground chia seeds mixed with ¼ cup (60 ml) water
- 1 teaspoon olive oil + 1 tablespoon (15 ml) water, for brushing loaf

In large mixing bowl, sift together the brown rice flour, cornstarch, psyllium husk, baking powder, and salt.

In a smaller bowl, mix the yeast with the sugar, warm water, and 1½ cups (355 ml) of the almond milk until foamy and let rest about 5 minutes. Add the water, vinegar, olive oil, and chia gel mixture.

Stir the wet ingredients into the flour mix. Add the remaining ½ cup (120 ml) almond milk. If using an electric mixer, mix on medium-high for about 2 minutes. If doing by hand, vigorously mix together the ingredients until a sticky dough forms and then continue to mix for 1 to 2 minutes until the dough becomes slightly fluffy.

Place in a lightly oiled standard-size loaf pan. Let rise in a warm place for about 50 minutes.

Preheat the oven to 400°F (200°C, gas mark 6). Lightly brush a mixture of olive oil and water onto the tops of the loaves. Bake on the middle rack for about 40 to 45 minutes or until golden brown on top. Let cool for 20 minutes before removing from the pan and let cool completely before cutting with a serrated knife.

RECIPE NOTE

To make easy and delicious homemade croutons, make a rub mixed with 1 teaspoon each dried rosemary, garlic powder, and onion powder. Lightly brush a few slices of bread, both front and back, with some softened vegan margarine. Rub the spice mixture on each side, cut into even squares, and bake on an ungreased baking sheet at 350°F (180°C, gas mark 4) for about 15 minutes, flipping once halfway through baking.

CHOPPED ENDIVE, "ROQUEFORT," PECAN, AND CRANBERRY SALAD

Sweet, salty, bitter, and sour come together tastefully in this colorful salad. To quickly toast the pecans in this recipe, simply place pecans on an ungreased baking sheet and roast in a preheated oven at 375°F (190°C, gas mark 5) for 5 to 7 minutes or until fragrant.

•   YIELD: 4 SMALL SIDE SALADS   •

FOR THE ROQUEFORT:

1 block (about 14 ounces, or 400 g) extra-firm tofu, pressed, see instructions below

3 teaspoons (16 g) white or yellow miso

3 tablespoons (45 ml) white wine

2 tablespoons (28 ml) lemon juice

3 tablespoons (45 ml) water

½ tablespoon Dijon mustard

FOR THE DRESSING:

2 tablespoons (30 g) Dijon mustard

1 tablespoon (20 g) agave

1 tablespoon (15 ml) lemon juice

2 teaspoons strawberry preserves

1 tablespoon (15 ml) water

FOR THE SALAD:

1¼ pounds (630 g, or about 5 heads), endive leaves cut into halves

1 cup (100 g) toasted pecans, chopped

1 cup (120 g) dried cranberries

TO MAKE THE ROQUEFORT: Make sure that your tofu is very well pressed so that practically all the water is removed. I like to press mine for 4 hours or more. To easily press tofu, drain all water from the package and then wrap the tofu tightly in a large, clean kitchen towel. Place the tofu on a flat baking sheet or plate and then top with another flat baking sheet or plate. Weigh down the tofu with a few heavy cans (two 30-ounce [840 g] cans of tomatoes work great) for 1 to 2 hours until most of the water from the tofu has been absorbed into the towel. Set aside.

Whisk together the miso, white wine, lemon juice, water, and mustard until smooth. Place the drained, pressed tofu in a small dish along with the miso mixture and let marinate 5 hours or up to overnight.

Preheat the oven to 225°F (110°C, gas mark ¼).

Drain the marinade from the tofu by pressing gently with your hands using a clean towel, just long enough to remove any excess liquid, and then cube into about 40 small pieces. Place the tofu in an ungreased baking dish and bake for 45 minutes, flipping halfway through. Refrigerate before using.

TO MAKE THE DRESSING: Whisk all the ingredients for the dressing together until they are smooth, but leave chunks of strawberries from the preserves remaining.

TO MAKE THE SALAD: Toss the dressing with endive leaves and then top with crushed pecans and cranberries and finally the Roquefort. Divide into 4 portions.

CAPRI SALAD WITH PINE NUTS OVER ARUGULA

This is a traditional take on the classic Capri salad. Use vegan mozzarella wedges or sliceable vegan cheese if you can find it, such as Follow Your Heart brand or Daiya Wedges. Otherwise, shredded vegan cheese works well if placed carefully on the stacks and broiled.

• • • • • • • • • • • • • • • • •   YIELD: 2 LARGE SALADS   • • • • • • • • • • • • • • • • •

2 large heirloom tomatoes

About 6 thick slices of vegan mozzarella-style cheese

1 tablespoon (15 ml) balsamic vinegar

1 tablespoon (15 ml) olive oil

½ teaspoon black pepper

Pine nuts to top

10 basil leaves

Handful of arugula

Slice the tomatoes into about three or four ½-inch (1 cm) thick slices. Stack the slices with a thin slice of vegan mozzarella in between each tomato slice, ending with a slice of cheese on top. All together you should have about 3 slices of tomato layered with 3 slices of cheese. Place under the broiler for about 4 minutes or until cheese bubbles and browns on top.

Drizzle with a little balsamic vinegar and olive oil. Top with black pepper and pine nuts. Serve over arugula leaves and garnish with basil.

RECIPE NOTE

Even though most of the world regards tomatoes as the crux of Italian cuisine, they weren't actually introduced to the country until the 1500s; however, Italy was the first place outside of South America to cultivate the plant. Directly after the Italian Renaissance (which spanned the fourteenth to sixteenth centuries), the cuisine of Italy had a rebirth with the introduction of the tomato.

ROASTED FENNEL SALAD WITH CARAMELIZED ONIONS

Much like a wilted spinach salad, the warmth of the caramelized onions in the dressing wilts the greens softly, while the bright notes of roasted fennel liven the salad and give it a good bit of depth.

YIELD: 4 SERVINGS

- 1 bulb fennel, cut into bite-size chunks
- 1 teaspoon olive oil, divided
- 1¼ teaspoons sea salt, divided
- 1 large Vidalia onion, sliced very thin
- 4 to 5 cups (120 to 150 g) fresh spinach
- 2 teaspoons lemon juice
- ½ teaspoon black pepper
- 1 apple, very thinly sliced into half moons
- 2 teaspoons flaxseed or chia seeds
- ½ cup (30 g) cut-up fennel greens (the feathery greens), chopped

Preheat the oven to 400°F (200°C, gas mark 6). Line a baking sheet with parchment paper and evenly place the fennel bulb pieces in a single layer on the baking sheet. Drizzle lightly with ½ teaspoon olive oil and ½ teaspoon sea salt. Bake for about 30 to 35 minutes or until tender and golden brown on the edges.

While the fennel is roasting, caramelize the Vidalia onion. In a small frying pan combine the onion with ½ teaspoon sea salt and the remaining ½ teaspoon olive oil and sauté over high heat until the edges turn brown and the onion begins to turn translucent, about 7 minutes. Reduce the heat slightly and continue sautéing until the onions begin to turn brown, about 7 more minutes. Reduce the heat once again and let cook, on about medium heat for about 5 more minutes, stirring often, until onions have transformed into a deep caramel brown and are very tender. Set aside to allow to cool briefly.

In a small bowl, toss together the caramelized onion, mixed greens, remaining sea salt, lemon juice, and black pepper and gently massage into the mixed greens just long enough to slightly wilt the leaves, about 15 to 30 seconds. Toss in the roasted fennel and apple, flax or chia seeds, and fennel greens.

RECIPE NOTE

This recipe works beautifully with other tender-leafed greens if you're up for a more adventurous recipe beyond spinach. Try using arugula, curly endive, baby bok choy leaves, or even beet greens cut into small pieces.

LEMON RICE SOUP

This deliciously creamy soup is inspired by a traditional
Greek soup called Avgolemono that features lemon and is thickened by egg.
In this vegan version, egg is replaced with gram flour (see page 13
for more information) to thicken and add depth to the soup.

•   YIELD: 6 SERVINGS   •

**½ cup (120 ml) lemon juice
(fresh squeezed is best)**

Zest of 1 lemon

2 cloves garlic, minced

1 sweet onion, diced

2 small stalks celery, thinly sliced

6 cups (1.4 L) vegetable broth

**¼ cup (30 g) gram flour, mixed
with ¼ cup (60 ml) water until
very smooth**

1 cup (158 g) cooked white rice

½ cup (30 g) fresh chopped parsley

6 lemon wedges

In a medium-size soup pot, combine the lemon juice and zest,
garlic, onion, celery, and vegetable broth and bring to a boil.
Reduce the heat and simmer until the onions are soft, about
20 minutes.

Slowly whisk in the gram flour paste and stir well to prevent
any lumps from forming. Stir in the rice and simmer for 10 to 15
minutes or until the soup thickens. Fold in the chopped parsley
and let cool about 10 minutes before serving. Garnish with
lemon wedges.

RECIPE NOTE

Lemons are such an integral part of Greek cuisine, you'll be hard
pressed to find many Greek recipes that don't include them,
whether sweet or savory. They perfectly complement the flavor of
olive oil—another object of Greek infatuation—and are featured
in everything from soups such as this one to sauces, pastas,
beverages, cakes, cookies, and more. Lemon halves are also
offered as edible garnish with almost every meal.

RED POTATO AND WATERCRESS SOUP

I am head over heels in love with this soup. Its red potato base gives it an undeniably familiar taste for anyone who loves potato soup, while the watercress adds a crisp note and fresh green color to the presentation.

•   YIELD: 6 SERVINGS   •

6 small red potatoes (1 pound, or 455 g), cubed

3 scallions, chopped

2 cloves garlic, minced

6 cups (1.4 L) water

1 teaspoon freshly ground black pepper

2 to 3 teaspoons sea salt, divided

2 large handfuls (10 to 15 g) watercress, chopped

Coconut cream (the thick part from the top of a can of coconut milk), for drizzling

In a large pot, combine the red potatoes, scallions, garlic, water, black pepper, and 1 teaspoon salt and bring to a boil. Once boiling, reduce to medium heat and let simmer until potatoes are easy to smash with a bit of pressure under a fork, about 8 to 9 minutes. Toss in watercress and cook an additional 1 to 2 minutes. Stir in an additional 1 teaspoon sea salt and blend using an immersion blender or cool slightly and transfer to a blender. Blend until fairly smooth, making sure to leave some tiny bits of watercress floating throughout.

Add up to 1 teaspoon sea salt to taste. Garnish with a drizzle of coconut cream before serving. This is best if served when slightly cooled, not piping hot.

RECIPE NOTE

This soup is not only irresistible in the taste department, but good for you, too! Watercress is a nutritional powerhouse, high in vitamin C, A, folic acid, and iron. It's even believed to have cancer-protecting properties and has been used for ages to prevent scurvy. So eat up!

ROASTED TOMATO AND BEET BISQUE

If you love borscht and tomato soup, you will adore this simple yet complex-tasting bisque. For a lighter soup, feel free to replace the coconut cream with $1/2$ cup (120 ml) vegetable broth.

• • • • • • • • • • • • • • • • • •   YIELD: 4 SERVINGS   •

2 medium-size tomatoes

1 large beet, peeled and sliced

2 cloves garlic

Salt, to taste

$1/2$ teaspoon olive oil

$1/2$ cup (120 ml) coconut cream

3 cups (700 ml) salted vegetable broth

Sea salt and black pepper to taste

Preheat the oven to 400°F (200°C, gas mark 6) and place a large piece of foil on top of a baking sheet.

Place the whole tomatoes, sliced beets, and garlic on foil and fold up the edges to create an open pouch around the vegetables. Salt lightly and drizzle with olive oil. Loosely close the pouch and bake in the preheated oven for about 1 hour or until the beets are tender.

Combine the roasted beets and tomatoes with the coconut cream in a food processor and blend until smooth. Add vegetable broth to thin and then salt and black pepper to taste. Transfer to a saucepan and warm gently before serving until the desired serving temperature is reached.

BORN-AGAIN BEET LOVER!

I used to not care for beets until I created this recipe. In fact, this soup changed my husband's perception about the brightly hued root veggies as well. The tomato really helped mellow out the earthy elements of the beet for me and opened my taste buds up to new beetly adventures! So, if you're not a beet lover, this soup may just be the recipe to convert you.

TRÉS TAPAS: PATATAS BRAVAS, STUFFED OLIVES, GARLIC MUSHROOMS

Tapas are a variety of small snacks, or appetizers, served in Spain and oftentimes ordered in groups. They can be served either warm or cold. The small "bite-size" nature of the dishes is thought to encourage conversation among diners—much like finger foods served at parties.

• •

FOR THE PATATAS BRAVAS SAUCE:

1 tablespoon (15 ml) olive oil
1 teaspoon chile pepper powder, or 1 whole small spicy red chile
2 cloves garlic, minced
1 small onion, diced
1 teaspoon sea salt
1 can (15 ounces, or 425 g) stewed tomatoes
2 teaspoons agave
1 teaspoon smoked paprika
1 tablespoon (16 g) tomato paste

FOR THE PATATAS:

3 large yellow-skinned potatoes
Salted water for boiling
Vegetable oil for frying

TO MAKE THE PATATAS BRAVAS SAUCE: Heat the olive oil in a medium-size frying pan. Sauté the chile pepper, garlic, onion, and salt over medium-high heat for about 10 minutes or until the onions are golden brown, stirring often. Reduce heat to medium low and add tomatoes, agave, smoked paprika, and tomato paste. Allow to simmer for about 10 minutes or until flavors have melded and sauce is fragrant.

TO MAKE THE PATATAS: Bring a large stockpot of water filled ⅔ of the way full to a rolling boil. Cut each potato into 1-inch (2.5 cm) cubes, drop in the pot, and cook for 3 to 4 minutes. Remove from the water and pat dry with a clean dish towel.

Preheat your deep fryer to 360°F (182°C). Once the oil is hot, deep-fry the potatoes for 7 to 8 minutes or until crispy and deep golden brown. Place on a paper towel or paper bag to drain any excess oil, salt lightly, and then place on a plate and smother with bravas sauce. Eat with toothpicks or small appetizer forks.

• • • • • • • YIELD: 6 SERVINGS • • • • • • •

FOR THE STUFFED OLIVES:

1 cup (110 g) crumbled Soyrizo (page 103)
2 tablespoons (12 g) nutritional yeast
16 colossal-size black olives, pits removed
Olive oil, for drizzling

Mix the Soyrizo with the 2 tablespoons (12 g) nutritional yeast. Spoon to fill the cavity of each olive. Place stuffed olives upright on a plate and drizzle with a thin stream of olive oil. Serve at room temperature.

• • • • YIELD: 16 OLIVE APPETIZERS • • •

FOR THE GARLIC MUSHROOMS:

2 tablespoons (28 ml) olive oil
20 ounces (560 g) fresh white button mushrooms, halved if large, left whole if bite size
5 cloves garlic, minced
½ cup (30 g) finely chopped packed fresh parsley, divided
1 small onion, minced
1 teaspoon sea salt

Heat the olive oil in a large frying pan over medium-high heat. Sauté the mushrooms, garlic, ¼ cup (15 g) parsley, onion, and salt, stirring often. Remove from the heat when the mushrooms are tender and the onions are translucent, about 10 to 15 minutes. Stir in the remainder of the parsley and sauté just to wilt the parsley.

Serve at room temperature.

• • • • • • • YIELD: 4 SERVINGS • • • • • • •

BOEUF(LESS) BOURGUIGNON

In case you are unfamiliar with postmodern-era cooking, my hero Julia Child made the classic recipe for boeuf bourguignon a household name in the 1960s when she revolutionized the kitchens of America with her tome *Mastering the Art of French Cooking*. This recipe is an animal-free version of the classic dish, and I think it fashionable enough to serve even to a party full of steak enthusiasts.

YIELD: 8 servings

FOR THE MARINADE:

- 1 tablespoon (2.4 g) fresh thyme
- ⅓ cup (80 ml) vegan Worcestershire sauce
- 2 cups (475 ml) vegetable broth (preferably beef flavored)
- 7 drops liquid smoke
- 1 package (8 ounces, or 225 g) Butler Soy Curls
- 3 tablespoons (45 g) vegan margarine
- ¼ cup (20 g) bacon-flavored bits
- Herb bouquet *(bouquet garni)*: sprigs of parsley, sage, rosemary, and thyme tied with kitchen twine

FOR THE SAUTÉ:

- 5 ounces (140 g) crimini or button mushrooms, halved
- 4 medium-size carrots, sliced into rounds
- 1 small red onion, diced
- 2 cloves garlic, minced
- 1 tablespoon (14 g) vegan margarine
- ½ teaspoon sea salt

FOR THE SAUCE:

- 3 tablespoons (30 g) superfine brown rice flour
- 1 teaspoon or 1 cube vegetable bouillon (beef flavored recommended)
- ½ cup (120 ml) full-bodied red wine, such as Zinfandel or Cabernet Sauvignon
- 1½ tablespoons (24 g) tomato paste
- 2 cups (475 ml) vegetable broth
- 10 small pearl onions, peeled but left whole

Preheat the oven to 350°F (180°C, gas mark 4).

TO MAKE THE MARINADE: Combine the marinade ingredients in a medium-size saucepan, bring just to a light boil, and then remove from the heat. In a large bowl, combine the marinade and Soy Curls and let rest for 15 minutes. Let the mixture come back down to room temperature and then using clean hands, squeeze out all the liquid from the Soy Curls, reserving the marinade in the bowl.

Place a large frying pan over medium-high heat and add the margarine and bacon bits. Sauté just until the bacon bits start to sizzle, about 5 minutes. Gently tilt the pan to evenly coat with bacon flavored margarine. Add the Soy Curls and sauté over medium-high heat until evenly browned, about 10 minutes. Transfer to a large casserole dish and add the bouquet of herbs.

TO MAKE THE SAUTÉ: Using the same saucepan the Soy Curls were cooked in, sauté the mushrooms, carrots, red onion, and garlic with about 1 tablespoon (14 g) margarine over medium-high heat, about 10 minutes or until the onions are translucent and lightly brown on the edges. Salt evenly while cooking.

TO MAKE THE SAUCE: Whisk the brown rice flour, bouillon, red wine, tomato paste, and vegetable broth into the leftover marinade, making sure no lumps remain in the liquid. Add the pearl onions.

Combine the cooked veggies with the Soy Curls in the casserole dish and then evenly top with sauce. Cover with foil and cook in the preheated oven for 1 hour. Uncover and cook an additional 25 minutes or until fragrant and bubbly on top. Remove the herb bouquet before serving.

Serve over mashed potatoes.

PASTA DA FORNEL

This is a vegan version of a dish from Northern Italy that features chopped lasagna noodles, dried fruit, poppy seeds, and Parmesan cheese.

•••••••   YIELD: 6 SERVINGS   •••••••

1½ cups (180 g) chopped walnuts
1 cup (150 g) dried figs
½ cup (120 ml) white wine
16 ounces (455 g) brown rice pasta
  (Tinkyada brand is recommended)
2 tablespoons (28 ml) olive oil
½ teaspoon sea salt
2 unpeeled apples, diced
1 small red onion, chopped
1 tablespoon (9 g) poppy seeds
½ cup (50 g) vegan Parmesan Cheese Mix,
  recipe at right
7 tablespoons (98 g) vegan margarine
Sea salt and black pepper to taste

Preheat the oven to 375°F (190°C, gas mark 5). Place the walnuts on a baking sheet and toast for 5 to 8 minutes. Remove and reserve for later.

Coarsely chop the figs and soak in the white wine for 4 hours or up to overnight.

Cook the pasta according to package directions. Drain and rinse briefly in cold water, return to the pan, and then stir in 2 tablespoons (28 ml) of olive oil and ½ teaspoon sea salt to coat the pasta.

Drain the figs. In a medium-size frying pan over medium-high heat, sauté the soaked figs, apples, and onion until the onion caramelizes, about 10 to 15 minutes.

Stir the fruit and the onions into the prepared pasta and then warm over low heat. Stir in the poppy seeds, vegan Parmesan, margarine, and walnuts and warm over medium heat until the margarine is melted and the Parmesan is well incorporated, stirring occasionally. Add sea salt to taste and black pepper.

PARMESAN CHEESE MIX

This recipe for Parmesan cheese resembles the kind that you can find in a shaker and can be added to numerous recipes or simply sprinkled on top of various dishes. I especially love this added to the very top of the Farinata Pizza (page 95) right before baking the second time around.

•••••••   YIELD: 2 CUPS (450 G)   •••••••

1½ cups (168 g) blanched almond meal
2 teaspoons sea salt
⅓ cup (32 g) nutritional yeast

Combine all the ingredients by shaking them together, about 30 shakes, in a large, airtight container. This keeps up to 1 month if stored in the refrigerator.

FLAVOR SAVOR:

Add a little oomph to your Parmesan cheese by placing a sprig of fresh rosemary, thyme, or oregano into the container when storing. For a delicate herb-Parmesan topping, let rest for one week and remove.

VEGGIE FRITTATA WITH SALSA VERDE

This quick frittata is one of the most requested dishes in my household. It can easily have countless variations by using seasonal vegetables from your local farmer's market in place of the ones listed. Try shredded kale instead of asparagus and zucchini in place of the carrot for a fun twist or try adding minced red pepper for a dash of color.

YIELD: 1 FRITTATA

FOR THE FRITTATA:

- **1 tablespoon (15 ml) olive oil**
- **6 stalks fresh asparagus, tough ends removed and chopped into ½-inch (1 cm) pieces**
- **1 medium-size red onion, diced**
- **2 cloves garlic, minced**
- **Dash salt**
- **1¾ cups (210 g) gram flour**
- **1 cup (235 ml) water**
- **1½ teaspoons sea salt**
- **¼ cup (24 g) nutritional yeast**
- **⅓ cup (80 ml) olive oil**
- **2 packages (12 ounces each, or a total of about 680 g) extra-firm tofu, drained and pressed for at least 4 hours or overnight**
- **Additional sea salt, to taste**
- **½ cup (55 g) packed shredded carrot**
- **½ cup (30 g) packed chopped fresh parsley**

FOR THE SALSA VERDE:

- **4 tomatillos**
- **1 Serrano chile pepper, diced**
- **4 shallots, peeled**
- **Giant handful fresh cilantro**
- **Half of a ripe avocado, peeled and pitted**
- **½ to ¾ teaspoon sea salt, to taste**

TO MAKE THE FRITTATA: Preheat your oven to 350°F (180°C, gas mark 4) and lightly grease a standard-size pie pan. Set aside.

Heat the olive oil in a small frying pan over medium heat. Add the asparagus, red onion, garlic, and a dash of salt and sauté gently until the asparagus turns a bright green and is barely tender, about 2 to 3 minutes.

In a large mixing bowl, whisk together the gram flour, water, sea salt, nutritional yeast, and olive oil to make a somewhat runny, yet substantial, batter. Crumble the blocks of tofu on top of the batter and salt lightly but evenly. Stir well to combine, but use a gentle touch so as not to purée the crumbled tofu.

Fold in the asparagus mixture, shredded carrot, and chopped parsley and then spread into the prepared pie pan. Bake for about 60 minutes or until golden brown on top. Remove from the oven and let cool at least 30 minutes before slicing. Top with the salsa verde and serve either warm or cold.

TO MAKE THE SALSA VERDE: Peel, wash, and roughly chop the tomatillos. Carefully deseed the Serrano pepper while wearing kitchen-grade gloves to prevent burning of the skin. Very roughly chop the shallots and place all the ingredients in a food processor. Pulse a few times until well combined to a salsa consistency. Add sea salt to taste. Store in an airtight container in the fridge.

SAVE THE FISHIES CAKES

Jackfruit and chickpeas create a texture for these cakes that is flaky, tender, undeniably delicious, and pretty similar in taste to a traditional fish cake thanks to the addition of dulse flakes. Top with tomato sauce (authentically British) or tartar sauce (American fusion).

YIELD: 12 CAKES

1 tablespoon (15 ml) olive oil

1 can (10 ounces, or 280 g) green jackfruit

1 tablespoon (3 g) dulse flakes

1 teaspoon minced fresh sage

1 teaspoon minced fresh thyme

1 teaspoon minced fresh tarragon

Additional salt, to taste

1½ cups (360 g) cooked chickpeas

1 large unpeeled potato, baked and chopped

½ cup (30 g) chopped fresh parsley

1 stalk celery, minced

2 to 3 dashes liquid smoke

1 teaspoon sea salt

½ teaspoon Dijon mustard

4 shallots, minced

2 tablespoons (20 g) superfine brown rice flour

Additional olive oil as needed

Preheat the oven to 400°F (200°C, gas mark 6).

Heat the olive oil in a frying pan over medium-high heat. Combine the jackfruit with the dulse flakes in the pan and sauté, stirring often, until the jackfruit becomes stringy and slightly golden brown, about 10 to 12 minutes. Toss in the sage, thyme, and tarragon and salt lightly while cooking. You may need to coax it into smaller strands with a plastic spatula while cooking. If it sticks slightly to your pan, add more oil.

In a blender, combine the sautéed jackfruit with the chickpeas and pulse carefully just until it becomes slightly crumbly. Transfer to a medium-size bowl and mash with the baked potato using a fork just until well combined.

Stir in the parsley, celery, liquid smoke, sea salt, Dijon, and shallots and combine until uniform. Lightly dust the dough with the brown rice flour, distributing evenly.

Shape into 3-inch (7.5 cm) patties and place on a parchment-lined or silicone mat-lined baking sheet. Brush both sides of each patty with olive oil and bake for 25 minutes. Flip and bake an additional 15 to 20 minutes or until the patties are golden brown on both sides.

RECIPE NOTE

To make a quick tartar sauce, simply combine ½ cup (115 g) vegan mayo with 1 tablespoon (15 g) dill relish and about ½ teaspoon lemon zest.

ENGLISH COTTAGE PIE

Also known as shepherd's pie in other parts of the world, this is a classic dish that was created to utilize leftovers. I never have any leftover mashed potatoes in my house, as I tend to devour them quite soon after making them, so I've included a recipe for those as well. Feel free to use your own leftover mashed potatoes to cut down on prep time with this recipe.

•   YIELD: 10 SERVINGS   •

FOR THE MEAT MIXTURE:

1 tablespoon (15 ml) olive oil

1 large sweet onion, diced

3 cloves garlic, minced

2 carrots, diced

2 stalks celery, diced

1 teaspoon fennel seed

½ teaspoon dried sage

2 cups (192 g) TVP (textured vegetable protein)

2 cups (475 ml) boiling water

2 cubes (2 teaspoons) beef-flavored vegetable bouillon

1 tablespoon (15 ml) vegan Worcestershire sauce

1 tablespoon (15 ml) olive oil

1 cup (164 g) corn kernels, thawed if frozen

2 cups (260 g) peas, thawed if frozen

1 tablespoon (12 g) ground chia seeds mixed with ½ cup (120 ml) water

FOR THE MASHED POTATOES:

5 large yellow-skinned potatoes, cubed into 1-inch (2.5 cm) squares

2 tablespoons (28 g) vegan margarine

1½ teaspoons sea salt (or to taste)

3 to 4 tablespoons (45 to 60 ml) almond milk

Preheat the oven to 375°F (190°C, gas mark 5). For the mashed potatoes, set a large pot of salted water on to boil.

To MAKE THE MEAT MIXTURE: Add the olive oil to a frying pan over medium-high heat. Add the onion, garlic, carrots, celery, fennel, and sage and sauté until browned, about 10 to 12 minutes.

In a large bowl, combine the TVP, boiling water, bouillon cubes, and Worcestershire sauce and cover for about 10 minutes or until all the water has been absorbed. Fluff with a fork and then toss into the frying pan with the vegetables. Add olive oil and cook until lightly browned, about 7 minutes. Stir in the corn.

Remove from the heat and add the chia seed mixture until well combined. Press into a 9 x 13-inch (23 x 33 cm) pan. Top with the peas.

To MAKE THE MASHED POTATOES: Once the water is boiling, gently add the cubed potatoes and bring back up to a rolling boil. Time for 13 minutes, or until fork tender, and then drain.

Transfer to an electric mixing bowl and add the margarine, sea salt, and 3 tablespoons (45 ml) almond milk. Mix until fluffy. The potatoes should be creamy, so add a touch more almond milk if needed. Spread potatoes on top of the peas, forming a smooth top layer. Using a fork, draw a few squiggles into the potatoes.

Bake for about 30 minutes or until the potatoes are browned on top.

BAKED PIEROGI WITH DILLED SOUR CREAM

This recipe is a combination of traditional pierogi mixed with pastry and portability. The result is a flaky, cheesy pocket pie, which has become a new favorite of mine. To make dilled sour cream, mix 1 tablespoon (4 g) minced dill leaves with ½ cup (115 g) vegan sour cream. Flavor with sea salt and lime juice to taste.

• • • • • • • • • • • • • • •   YIELD: 20 PIEROGIES   • • • • • • • • • • • • • • •

FOR THE PASTRY:

2 cups (320 g) superfine brown rice flour

1 cup (112 g) almond meal/flour

2 teaspoons xanthan gum

¼ cup (51 g) sweet white rice flour

¼ cup (30 g) tapioca flour

½ cup (85 g) potato starch

1 teaspoon baking powder

7 tablespoons (98 g) cold vegan margarine

¾ cup (175 ml) plus 2 tablespoons (28 ml) ice-cold water

½ tablespoon ground chia seeds mixed with 2 tablespoons (28 ml) water

FOR THE FILLING:

1 tablespoon (15 ml) olive oil for cooking

1 Vidalia onion, chopped

Dash sea salt

3 large baked yellow potatoes

1 teaspoon additional sea salt

1 tablespoon (14 g) vegan margarine

¾ cup (90 g) shredded Cheddar-style vegan cheese

Fresh cracked black pepper

TO MAKE THE PASTRY: In a large bowl, whisk together the superfine brown rice flour, almond flour, xanthan gum, sweet white rice flour, tapioca flour, potato starch, and baking powder. Use a pastry blender to cut in the margarine until it forms into even crumbles.

Make a well in the center of the flour and stir in the ice-cold water with a fork and then stir in the chia seed mixture. Combine into a dough, knead a few times, and separate into 2 disks. Wrap in waxed paper and chill while you make the filling.

TO MAKE THE FILLING: Add the olive oil to a skillet and heat over medium-high heat. Add the Vidalia onion and a dash of sea salt and sauté until browned, about 10 minutes. Reduce the heat slightly and cook until soft and deep golden brown, about 10 minutes. Transfer to a bowl and combine with the potatoes, sea salt, and margarine and mash with a potato masher or very large fork until smooth. Stir in the nondairy cheese and black pepper. Let cool.

TO ASSEMBLE: Preheat the oven to 375°F (190°C, gas mark 5). Roll out the pastry dough to about ¼-inch (6 mm) thickness between 2 sheets of plastic wrap. Using an inverted cereal-size bowl, cut out circular shapes and place 2 tablespoons (28 g) filling on half of the circle. Flip over half of the dough to form half-moon shapes and press down with a fork to crimp and seal edges. Cut 1-inch (2.5 cm) slits into the tops and drizzle lightly with olive oil. Bake for 30 minutes. Increase the oven temperature to 400° F (200°C, gas mark 6) and bake an additional 10 minutes until golden brown and crispy. Serve immediately with dilled sour cream, recipe above.

SUGARED SPANISH ALMONDS

A popular treat in the streets of Spain, it's hard to argue with the intoxicating flavor of these candies. These keep well if kept in an airtight container or loosely wrapped paper bag, but honestly, they have never actually lasted very long around my house.

• YIELD: 3 CUPS (550 G) CANDIED NUTS • • • • • • • • • • • • • • • • •

1 ½ cups (300 g) granulated sugar

½ cup (120 ml) + 2 tablespoons (28 ml) water

Pinch salt

Half vanilla bean, scraped

2 ½ cups (363 g) whole raw almonds

Line a baking sheet with waxed paper.

In 2-quart (2 L) saucepan, combine the sugar, water, salt, and vanilla bean and bring to a boil over medium heat, stirring often with a wooden spoon.

Once the mixture comes to a boil, add the almonds and set your timer for 16 minutes, keeping the mixture at a boil. Stirring continuously, let the syrup in the mix completely recrystallize into sugar granules. This should happen at around the 10-minute mark. Continue stirring, and by the time the 16 minutes is up, the sugar should have mostly turned back into a syrup to coat the individual almonds.

Remove from the heat just as the sugar turns back into a glaze and spread onto the waxed paper–covered baking sheet. Separate into individual almonds and let cool completely before serving.

RECIPE NOTE

Although Spain may be a vast producer of almonds, the sweet and fragrant nut originated in the Middle East and South Asia. When these confections are sold by street vendors in Spain, they are called *almendras garrapiñadas*.

FIG PASTRIES

This pastry is especially delicious when served with a fresh "sweetened cream," which can be made by mixing together equal parts vegan cream cheese and vegan sour cream, a touch of sugar, and a little lemon zest.

•   YIELD: 14 PASTRIES   •

FOR THE PASTRY:

1½ cups (240 g) superfine brown rice flour

¼ cup (51 g) sweet white rice flour

2 teaspoons xanthan gum

¼ cup (50 g) granulated sugar

½ cup (112 g) cold vegan margarine, chopped into 1-inch (2.5 cm) square pieces

½ cup (120 ml) ice-cold water

FOR THE FILLING:

1⅓ cup (200 g) dried mission figs

½ cup (115 g) packed dark brown sugar

2 teaspoons vegan margarine

Dash sea salt

2 dashes angostura bitters, optional

TO MAKE THE PASTRY: In a large bowl, mix together the flours, xanthan gum, and sugar until well blended. Using a pastry blender, cut the margarine into the flour mixture until it forms coarse crumbs. Make a well in the center. Use a fork to slowly stir the ice-cold water into the flour mixture just until it comes together into a dough. Quickly knead the dough a couple of times to form a disk. Wrap in waxed paper and chill in the refrigerator until cold, about 1 hour. In the meantime, prepare the filling.

TO MAKE THE FILLING: Dice the dried figs finely and combine with remaining filling ingredients. Smash using a large fork or potato masher, just so that the ingredients blend well. Large chunks of fruit remaining in some spots are desirable.

TO ASSEMBLE: Preheat the oven to 375°F (190° C, gas mark 5). Once the dough is cold, divide in half and roll out between 2 sheets of plastic wrap on a flat surface, creating a rectangle that is about ¼-inch (6 mm) thick from each half. Cut out 14 disks of dough, each about 2 inches (5 cm) in diameter (a small bowl works well as a cookie cutter here) for a total of 28 pieces of dough. Place about 1 heaping tablespoon (15 g) filling in the center of one circle and then cover with another circle of dough and crimp down the edges of the dough to seal.

Slice a slit into the tops of each pocket and bake on a parchment-covered cookie sheet for about 25 minutes or until very lightly golden brown on edges. Serve warm or cold with sweetened cream.

FUNDAMENTAL FIGS

Figs have been an important part of Greek and Sicilian cuisine since ancient times. Used not only as a dessert fruit, dried figs are also eaten as an appetizer or along with wine.

{ Chapter 4 }

TASTY TRAVELS TO SOUTH AND CENTRAL AMERICA

South America is home to many fruits, vegetables, and edible plants that have become modern-day staples around the world through exportation. Maize, potatoes, quinoa, cassava, peanuts, pineapples, cashews, and strawberries all originated here, with the continent sharing many of its native foodstuffs with Mexico and Central America. When Europeans arrived back in 1498, they introduced many of their European foods such as livestock, almonds, citrus, and wheat, influencing this continental cuisine in countless ways.

Today you will find an eclectic mix of flavors and foods in South American cuisine, including many potato- and grain-based dishes with heavy Spanish and Portuguese influence, especially in the regions around Brazil. One thing the entire continent seems to have in common, though, is its love for chile peppers. Whether eaten fresh, roasted, smoked, or ground, chiles are very much a part of South American cuisine, as you'll see in the following recipes.

Central America covers the areas basically in-between Mexico and South America. The prime real estate of this region made it a perfect place for the cultures of North America and South America to blend their cuisines and tastes. This food features many wonderful native dishes similar to South American cuisine, but with a few European twists thrown in for good measure. Plants such as sugarcane, chile peppers, plantains, and coconut grow abundantly and flavor the native fare. Right next door to Central America lie the Caribbean islands, which number in the thousands. The most familiar of these are probably Jamaica and the Bahamas, which are both home to a sort of fusion cuisine with primary influences from Europe, East Asia, and Africa.

FENNEL AND KALE CORN BREAD

Unlike American corn bread, which is rather sweet, this corn bread is deliciously savory and beautifully marbled with kale for both color and texture. Use finely ground cornmeal rather than coarsely ground to achieve a better texture and even cooking.

. . . . YIELD: 4 MINI LOAVES . . . .

- 1½ cups (210 g) yellow cornmeal
- ¾ cup (300 g) masa harina flour
- ½ cup (48 g) nutritional yeast
- 2 teaspoons fennel seeds
- 2 teaspoons baking powder
- 1 teaspoon sea salt
- 2 tablespoons (24 g) ground chia seeds mixed with 6 tablespoons (90 ml) water
- 1 cup (164 g) cooked corn kernels
- 2 cups (470 ml) nondairy milk
- ⅓ cup (80 ml) olive oil
- 1 cup (67 g) packed finely chopped kale

Preheat the oven to 350°F (180°C, gas mark 4). Lightly grease 4 mini loaf pans or a 9 x 11-inch (23 x 28 cm) baking dish.

In a large mixing bowl, combine the cornmeal, masa harina, nutritional yeast, fennel, baking powder, and sea salt. Make a well in the center of the flour and add the prepared chia seed, corn kernels, nondairy milk, and oil. Stir well to incorporate, and fold in the chopped kale.

Spread evenly into the prepared baking dish and bake for 40 to 60 minutes if baking mini loaves or 30 to 40 minutes if baking in a standard pan.

SWEET OR SAVORY

Translate this recipe easily to a sweeter version of corn bread by simply excluding the nutritional yeast and kale and replacing them with ⅓ cup (67 g) sugar and ¼ cup (41 g) more corn kernels. Follow the rest of the directions as indicated above.

RUSSIAN SALAD (ENSALADA RUSA)

Ensalada rusa is a potato-based salad that, like its name implies, has its origins in Russia. Over the years it has gained fans in Spain, Italy, and eventually made its way to South America, where it is standard daily fare in places such as Argentina and the surrounding areas and a welcome addition to the dinner table during the holidays.

• • • • • • • • • • • • • • • • •   YIELD: 8 SERVINGS   •

FOR THE DRESSING:

12 ounces (340 g) silken tofu, drained

1 tablespoon (15 g) spicy brown mustard

2 tablespoons (28 ml) apple cider vinegar

2 tablespoons (28 g) vegan mayonnaise

1 teaspoon sea salt

FOR THE SALAD:

3 medium-size Yukon gold potatoes, baked whole

½ cup (30 g) finely chopped, packed parsley

1 large carrot, shredded

¼ cup (60 g) dill relish

4 vegan hot dogs (make sure they're gluten-free, like Tofu Pups or Not Dogs), diced

4 slices American-style vegan cheese, stacked and diced

5 small shallots, sliced

1 tablespoon (2.4 g) fresh thyme

Sea salt and black pepper to taste

Make the dressing by placing all ingredients into a food processor or blender and blending until smooth, scraping down the sides as necessary.

Cube the baked potatoes into bite-size pieces, salt lightly, and then toss with the other salad ingredients. Gently fold in the dressing to fully coat. Salt and pepper to taste. Serve cold.

PERFECT POTATOES:

When baking potatoes, don't wrap them in aluminum foil or the skins will become soft instead of crispy. Bake them directly on the oven rack with a pan placed underneath, at 400°F (200°C, gas mark 6) for 45 to 50 minutes. Pierce with a fork to test for doneness.

BEETROOT SALAD

This delightful salad is as colorful as it is tasty, with an assortment of flavors from the earthy sweetness of roasted beets to the subtle bite of horseradish. It makes a perfect simple side salad for lunch or a light dinner when eaten alongside a bowl of Caribbean Black Bean Soup (page 89).

● ● ● ● ● ● ● ● ● ● ● ● ● ● ● ● ● ●   YIELD: 2 SIDE SALADS   ● ● ● ● ● ● ● ● ● ● ● ● ● ● ● ● ● ●

I medium-size beet

FOR THE DRESSING:

I teaspoon horseradish

3 tablespoons (42 g) vegan mayonnaise

½ tablespoon agave

FOR THE SALAD:

4 cups (80 g) baby arugula leaves, or (228) mixed greens

½ mango, cut into small pieces

¼ cup (36 g) toasted sunflower seeds

TO ROAST THE BEET: Preheat the oven to 375°F (190°C, gas mark 5).
Poke the beet on all sides with a fork, wrap loosely in foil, and bake for about 45 minutes or until fork tender. Set aside until cool and then peel and chop.

Whisk together the ingredients for the dressing and toss gently with the arugula leaves. Top with beet, mango, and sunflower seeds and serve.

FROM SALAD TO CENTERPIECE:

Make this side an easy main course by tossing with 4 cups (540 g) of piping hot brown rice pasta. The salad dressing will coat the noodles superbly, while the other ingredients act as colorful (and delicious) accents.

CARIBBEAN BLACK BEAN SOUP

This recipe is undeniably one of my favorite versions of black bean soup I've tasted. It's not creamy but more soup-like than the thick American staple and has a slightly sweet undertone from the brown sugar.

YIELD: 8 servings

- **1 tablespoon (15 ml) olive oil or (14g) coconut oil for sautéing**
- **1 red pepper, seeded and chopped**
- **1 cube ginger (1 inch [2.5 cm]), grated**
- **1 large red onion, diced**
- **8 ounces (225 g) mushrooms, quartered**
- **2 cloves garlic, diced**
- **1 teaspoon sea salt for sautéing**
- **1 teaspoon allspice**
- **1 jalapeño pepper, seeded and diced**
- **1 tablespoon (2.4 g) fresh thyme**
- **2 tablespoons (30 g) packed brown sugar**
- **5 cups (1 L) salted vegetable broth**
- **3½ cups (602 g) cooked black beans**
- **Additional sea salt (about ¾ teaspoon) for flavor, if needed**
- **3 scallions, chopped**

Heat the olive oil in a large stockpot over medium-high heat, add all the ingredients up to the brown sugar, and cook until the vegetables are tender, about 12 minutes, stirring often. Add the brown sugar and the rest of ingredients except the scallions and bring to a boil over medium-high heat. Reduce the heat and simmer 25 minutes. Salt to taste, if needed.

Serve topped with scallions.

WORLDLY FEAST!

Caribbean cuisine is a fusion of Native American, European, and African cuisine, with the addition of its own native flair. It's truly a melting pot of international cuisine!

PLANTAIN AND POTATO SOUP

This deliciously filling soup is much like traditional potato soup with the tropical addition of cooked plantains, which add a touch of sweetness.

·   YIELD: 6 SERVINGS   ·

2 medium-size yellow potatoes, cubed

1 large Vidalia onion, diced

2 cloves garlic, minced

2 large plantains, green with some brown spots, peeled and sliced into thick coins

2 dashes turmeric

6 cups (1.4 L) water

3 teaspoons (15 g) sea salt

Place the potatoes, onion, garlic, plantains, turmeric, and water in a pot. Bring to a boil and then reduce the heat slightly to a constant simmer. Add sea salt.

Simmer for 20 minutes after boiling and then remove half of the soup and place it in a blender or food processor. Blend until smooth and then return the puréed soup to the rest of the soup in the pot to combine.

Let cool slightly before serving.

A SPLASH OF COLOR!

My favorite addition to this soup is a sprinkle of smoked paprika—a bright red spice that no well-stocked pantry should ever be without.

POTATOES WITH SPICY CHILE CREAM SAUCE (HUANCAYO-STYLE)

These spicy potatoes are a popular dish that originates from a small province of Peru, and because they are typically served cold, they are a popular choice for picnics and potlucks. The zesty sauce for this dish also makes a delicious condiment for other foods. I love having a container of it in my refrigerator to enjoy with corn tortillas or even fresh vegetables such as celery and carrots.

• YIELD: 4 SERVINGS •

4 medium-size yellow potatoes
Olive oil for drizzling
I to 2 habanero peppers, deseeded
I large red bell pepper, halved
2 cloves garlic, minced
Additional olive oil for drizzling
Salt, to taste
I½ cups (144 g) nutritional yeast
I¼ cups (140 g) almond meal
Dash turmeric
½ cup (120 ml) coconut cream (the thick layer on top of a can of coconut milk)
I teaspoon sea salt
¼ cup (60 ml) olive oil
I¼ cups (205 ml) vegan milk, or to thin
Olives for garnish
Lettuce, optional

Preheat your oven to 400°F (200°C, gas mark 6).

You'll roast the potatoes, peppers, and garlic at the same time. Pierce the potatoes with a fork all over and then place on an ungreased baking sheet. Drizzle lightly with olive oil and place in the oven for 40 to 60 minutes or until fork tender. Remove from the oven once cooked through and let cool about 10 minutes before slicing into ¼-inch (6 mm) slices.

Line another baking sheet with foil and place the peppers and garlic on the sheet. Drizzle with olive oil, salt lightly, and loosely wrap the peppers with foil to make a roomy pouch. Roast for about 30 to 40 minutes or until the peppers are soft at the same time that the potatoes are cooked. Unwrap the peppers carefully, as the habaneros are really spicy and can get into your eyes if you stand too close or open too hastily.

Place the roasted peppers and garlic in a food processor or blender and add the nutritional yeast, almond meal, turmeric, coconut cream, sea salt, and olive oil. Blend until smooth, adding in small additions of nondairy milk to thin.

Cover the sliced potatoes with sauce. Garnish with olives and serve warm over a bed of lettuce.

MUSHROOM-PEPPER QUINOA RISOTTO

Risotto is traditionally made with Arborio or another short-grained rice, but this version, which uses the wonderful South African grain quinoa, is equally creamy and worth the extra steps to prepare. If you cannot find lemon verbena, substitute about a teaspoon of lemon zest.

YIELD: 6 SERVINGS

- **3 tablespoons (45 ml) olive oil**
- **I sweet onion, diced**
- **3 cups (210 g) cremini mushrooms, cut into chunks**
- **2 bell peppers (I yellow, I red), diced**
- **I teaspoon ground coriander**
- **I teaspoon fine sea salt**
- **1¼ cups (216 g) quinoa, rinsed**
- **½ cup (120 ml) gluten-free beer, slightly flat and room temperature**
- **3 cups (700 ml) salted vegetable broth, divided**
- **1½ cups (180 ml) coconut milk**
- **Sprinkle of paprika, for garnish**
- **3 to 4 leaves lemon verbena, whole or cut into fine chiffonade**

RECIPE NOTE

Make sure all liquid you add is at room temperature. Risotto is a dish that is much easier to cook when all your ingredients are prepared and ready to go ahead of time.

In a large frying pan, heat the olive oil over high heat. Add the diced onion, mushrooms, bell peppers, coriander, and sea salt. Stir often and cook for about 10 to 12 minutes until all moisture is removed from the vegetables and the mushrooms reduce in size. Drain any excess liquid and transfer to a bowl.

Reduce the heat to medium high. Add a drizzle more olive oil to the pan and the quinoa. Cook the quinoa, stirring often, until toasted and fragrant, about 2 minutes.

Reduce the heat again to medium low and carefully pour in the beer (you may want to step back from the pan, as the carbonation could cause a bubbly burst). Cook until all liquid is absorbed. Then, add 1 cup (235 ml) vegetable broth and cook, again stirring often, until most of the liquid has been absorbed. Add the coconut milk, in ½ cup (120 ml) increments, until all is used. Then add up to 2 cups (475 ml) more vegetable broth until the quinoa is tender. The entire process to cook the quinoa should take about 30 minutes—taste toward the end to make sure the quinoa is tender; it should have a slightly firm but soft texture when it is done. Be sure between each addition of liquid that the quinoa is fairly dry and not much liquid remains before adding in more. If the liquid is absorbing too quickly, reduce your heat slightly.

Stir in the mushrooms and peppers, sprinkle with paprika, and top with lemon verbena. Serve warm.

FARINATA PIZZA

Farinata is a crispy flatbread made from gram, or chickpea, flour. It is also known as *socca* in France and *cecina* in Italy. In many parts of South America, especially along the southern regions, traditional wheat-crusted pizza is enjoyed with a layer of farinata on the bottom. In this recipe I decided to leave out the regular pizza crust and feature only the farinata as the crust, as I have long been a fan of this naturally vegan and gluten-free pizza.

● YIELD: 1 PIZZA ●

FOR THE CRUST:

2 cups (240 g) gram flour

I teaspoon sea salt

¼ cup (60 ml) olive oil

I cup (235 ml) + 2 tablespoons (28 ml) water

FOR THE SAUCE:

6 ounces (170 g) tomato paste

½ tablespoon minced thyme

½ tablespoon minced oregano

2 cloves garlic, minced

I tablespoon (13 g) sugar

2 tablespoons (28 ml) olive oil

I tablespoon (15 ml) balsamic vinegar

Scant ½ cup (120 ml) water

FOR THE TOPPINGS:

2 cups (224 g) mozzarella-style shredded vegan cheese

I red onion, sliced very thin

6 button mushrooms, sliced very thin

½ cup (75 g) finely diced green pepper

Preheat the oven to 385°F (195°C, gas mark 6). Line a large jelly-roll or baking sheet with a silicone mat or parchment paper (a silicone mat produces a crisper crust).

In a large bowl, whisk together all the ingredients for the crust, getting rid of any and all lumps in the batter. Spread thinly on the baking sheet so that the batter is about ¼-inch (6 mm) thick. Bake for about 13 minutes. Remove the crust from the oven and increase the temperature to 450°F (230°C, gas mark 8).

Prepare the sauce by mixing together all the ingredients except the water. Slowly add the water and mix well to completely incorporate. Spread a thin layer of sauce onto the crust and then top with the toppings. I like the order of cheese, onions, mushrooms, and green peppers, but feel free to play around.

Bake the pizza for about 15 minutes or until the cheese is melted and the toppings begin to brown. Watch carefully so that it doesn't burn. Let cool briefly and then slice and serve.

RECIPE NOTE

I've included my favorite toppings to introduce you to this variety of crust, but feel free to add the toppings you love the most to this pizza. Slice any veggies you add very thinly so they cook completely while baking. Thicker toppings will often remain uncooked or unevenly cooked because they are in the oven only for a short time.

COLOMBIAN EMPANADAS

Empanadas are made in various ways all over South America, varying from savory to sweet and everything in between. This recipe uses a corn-based dough and has a vegetable filling that is traditional to Colombia.

•   YIELD: 12 EMPANADAS   •

FOR THE DOUGH:
2½ cups (560 g) masa harina flour
3 cups (700 ml) hot water
1½ teaspoons sea salt

FOR THE FILLING:
1 tablespoon (15 ml) olive oil
1 cup (70 g) chopped mushrooms
1 small potato, diced
1 onion, diced
1 clove garlic, minced
Salt, to taste
¼ cup (4 g) packed cilantro
1 cup (130 g) frozen peas, thawed
1 teaspoon cumin
¾ cup (84 g) vegan cheese shreds (Daiya brand works best)
Vegetable oil for frying

In a medium-size bowl, combine the masa harina, hot water, and salt into a dough using a fork. Cover and let rest about 20 minutes.

TO PREPARE THE FILLING: Heat the olive oil over medium-high heat in a large frying pan and sauté the mushrooms, potato, onion, and garlic until the potato is softened and the onions are translucent, about 10 to 15 minutes. Salt lightly while cooking.

Stir the cilantro, peas, cumin, and cheese shreds into the rest of the filling mixture. Transfer to a bowl and set in the refrigerator to cool.

TO ASSEMBLE THE EMPANADAS: Grab a touch larger than a golf-ball-size amount of dough and roll out in-between 2 pieces of plastic wrap, forming a 5-inch (13 cm) diameter circle. Place about 1 heaping tablespoon (15 g) of the filling on half of the dough and using the plastic wrap, gently coax the other half of the circle to cover the filling. Use your fingers to seal the dough and form a half moon–shaped pocket. Make sure there aren't any breaks or tears in the empanada; if needed, use wet fingers to help seal any small holes. Place prepared empanadas on a parchment-covered surface and repeat until all dough and filling has been used.

TO COOK THE EMPANADAS: Preheat a deep fryer to 360°F (182°C). Prepare a surface with either paper bags or paper towels to place the empanadas on once they have cooked.

Drop about 3 empanadas at a time into the preheated oil and cook for 6 minutes or until golden yellow in color. Place on the prepared surface and let cool briefly before serving.

RECIPE NOTE

For an easy alternate filling, simply stuff the empanadas with Soyrizo (page 103) and follow the directions the same way.

JAMAICAN JACKFRUIT PATTIES

Similar to empanadas, these patties are baked, not fried,
and feature the lovely bright yellow color and unique flavor
of turmeric in the dough.

• • • • • • • • • • • • • • • • • • •   YIELD: 12 PATTIES   • • • • • • • • • • • • • • • • • • •

FOR THE PASTRY:

1 cup (160 g) superfine brown rice flour

1 cup (136 g) sorghum flour

½ cup (96 g) potato starch

¼ cup (51 g) sweet white rice flour

¾ teaspoon sea salt

1 teaspoon xanthan gum

2 teaspoons turmeric

7 tablespoons (98 g) cold vegan margarine, chopped

1 cup (235 ml) very cold water

FOR THE FILLING:

2 tablespoons (28 ml) olive oil

1 can (10 ounces, or 280 g) green jackfruit

1 small red onion, minced

2 cloves garlic, minced

1 teaspoon sea salt

½ tablespoon ground chia seeds mixed with ¼ cup (60 ml) water

1 tablespoon (15 ml) vegan Worcestershire sauce (or Pickapeppa, or Salsa Lizano)

1 tablespoon (16 g) tomato paste

1 tablespoon (15 g) brown sugar

Few drops liquid smoke

Dash red pepper

1 teaspoon paprika

¼ cup (30 g) gluten-free bread crumbs

¼ cup (60 ml) water

TO MAKE THE PASTRY: In a large bowl, whisk together all the pastry ingredients except the margarine and cold water. Cut in the margarine using a pastry blender until the mixture is uniform and resembles coarse crumbs. Make a well in the center of the flour and stir in the cold water using a fork until all is combined. Pat into a patty and chill the dough for about 30 minutes.

TO MAKE THE FILLING: In a large frying pan, heat the olive oil over medium high, add the jackfruit, onion, garlic, and sea salt and sauté until the onions are translucent and the jackfruit starts to shred, about 12 minutes. You may need to use a wooden fork to get it to shred into thin pieces.

Add the chia mixture, Worcestershire sauce, tomato paste, brown sugar, liquid smoke, red pepper, and paprika and let simmer a few minutes until fragrant. Stir in the bread crumbs and the water and cook gently over medium heat until thickened, about 5 to 7 minutes. Cook an additional 2 minutes. Take off the heat and set aside.

TO ASSEMBLE: Preheat your oven to 375°F (190°C, gas mark 5). Roll out the dough in between 2 sheets of plastic wrap until about ⅕-inch (5 mm) thick. Using a small bowl (about 3 inches [7.5 cm] in diameter), cut 12 circle shapes out of the dough.

Place about 1 tablespoon's (15 g) worth of filling on half of the dough and then gently pull the other side of the dough over to cover. Seal by pressing down the edges of the dough with a fork. Place on an ungreased baking sheet and bake for 30 minutes or until golden brown and crispy on the edges. Serve hot.

PANAMANIAN TAMALES

Banana leaves, which lend a unique flavor to the tamales,
can be easily found frozen at Asian groceries and simply thawed
before using. Be sure they are de-ribbed before using and when
assembling, avoid folding against the ridges to prevent tearing.

• • • • • • • • • • • • • •   YIELD: 15 TAMALES   • • • • • • • • • • • • • •

FOR THE DOUGH:

I cup (224 g) vegan margarine

3 cups (680 g) masa harina

2¾ cups (650 ml) vegetable broth, warmed

FOR THE FILLING:

I tablespoon (15 ml) olive oil

5 cremini mushrooms, minced

I cup (120 g) zucchini, diced

I teaspoon cumin

I tablespoon (1 g) minced cilantro leaves, or fresh cilantro leaves (these are different spices, but similar in taste)

I small onion, diced

I clove garlic, minced

I teaspoon sea salt

½ cup (56 g) vegan cheese shreds (Daiya brand recommended)

5 large banana leaves, cut into 15 even-size squares, about 10 x 12 inches (25 x 30 cm) (Note: Use as much of the natural shape as possible to prevent shredding.)

FOR THE DOUGH: Cut the margarine into the masa harina using your hands or a pastry blender until uniform. Use a fork to stir in the vegetable broth and mix well. Let rest while you prepare the filling.

FOR THE FILLING: Add the olive oil to a large frying pan over medium-high heat and sauté all the ingredients except for the vegan cheese until all the vegetables are tender and onions are translucent and slightly browned on the edges, about 10 minutes. Stir in the vegan cheese, letting the pan remain over the heat, until the cheese has melted. Let cool slightly.

If the banana leaves are too tough to fold easily, blanch in boiling water for 1 minute.

TO ASSEMBLE THE TAMALES: Lay 1 banana leaf smooth side up onto a clean, flat surface. Press about 2 tablespoons (28 g) of masa harina mixture into the middle of the leaf, forming as close to a rectangle as possible. In the very center of the masa dough, place about 1 tablespoon (15 g) filling so that it stretches the length of the dough but remains in the very center. Roll up, trying to get each end of the tamale to touch and wrapping the banana leaf snugly so that it is water tight. I like to wrap it as I would a package: one end rolled up, sides turned in, holding it down to keep sealed. Tie tightly on 2 ends with kitchen twine to seal. Repeat with all the leaves until the dough has been used up.

Bring a very large pot of water to a rolling boil and carefully drop the tamales into the water. To prevent them from floating, I place a metal strainer on top of the pot to press the tamales down gently and then cover with an oversize lid. Let cook 1 hour over medium heat (remaining at a constant bubble) and then transfer to a wire rack for about 20 minutes. Unwrap carefully and enjoy!

SOY-RIPAN SANDWICHES

SOYRIZO

The classic choripán sandwich generally features chorizo, but the recipe for Soyrizo on the right is a great substitute for the traditional spicy sausage. You can also find prepackaged soyrizo in many grocery and natural foods markets.

•••••• YIELD: 1 SANDWICH ••••••

FOR THE CHIMICHURRI SAUCE:
½ cup (30 g) fresh parsley
3 tablespoons (12 g) fresh oregano
¼ cup (60 ml) olive oil
1 teaspoon sea salt
2 tablespoons (28 ml) lime juice
Paprika, to taste
1 to 2 tablespoons (15 to 28 ml) water to thin

FOR THE PAN-FRIED SOYRIZO:
1 tablespoon (15 ml) olive or coconut oil
½ cup (57 g) Soyrizo, crumbled (⅙ of the
   roll from recipe at right)

Whirl all the ingredients for the chimichurri sauce in a food processor until smooth like pesto.

Heat a small frying pan over medium-high heat. Add the oil and let warm up, about 30 seconds. Toss in the Soyrizo crumbles and stir often just to brown, about 5 to 7 minutes.

Spread the chimichurri sauce generously on top of 1 thick slice of Pain Ordinaire (page 51) or other gluten-free bread and top with pan-fried Soyrizo (recipe at right) and dill relish and then close with another thick slice of bread slathered with a thin coating of vegan mayonnaise.

YIELD: 1 ROLL SOYRIZO, ABOUT 3 CUPS (350 G)

1 tablespoon (15 ml) olive oil
2 to 3 cloves fresh garlic, finely minced
1 cup (96 g) TVP (textured vegetable protein)
1 cup (235 ml) boiling water
1 salted vegetable bouillon cube (1 teaspoon bouillon)
1 teaspoon red chile powder
1 teaspoon chile flakes
2 teaspoons powdered cumin
Few dashes liquid smoke
1 teaspoon sea salt
1 tablespoon (15 ml) olive oil
3 teaspoons (7 g) paprika
1 heaping tablespoon (6 g) nutritional yeast
1 teaspoon cumin seeds, toasted
1 teaspoon fennel seeds, toasted
1 teaspoon fresh cracker black pepper
1 tablespoon (12 g) ground chia seeds
   mixed with ¼ cup (60 ml) water

Place a small pan with olive oil over medium-high heat. Add the garlic and sauté briefly, about 30 seconds. Set aside.

In a medium-size bowl, dissolve the bouillon cube in the boiling water, mix the TVP into the boiling water, and let rest about 10 minutes, covered, until all the water has been absorbed. Fluff with a fork.

Stir in all the other ingredients in the order listed and work with your hands until very well combined. Form into a log on a sheet of plastic wrap and wrap tightly and then twist and tie the ends to seal. Let chill overnight to let the garlic and other flavors meld.

FRESH CORN FRITTERS

These crispy, crunchy treats are hard to beat when served with
a simple aioli sauce, which I've included a recipe for below.
For incredible fritters, use corn that has been just cut from the cob.
Haiti's native foods are similar to those of other Central American and
Caribbean countries. Its cooking differs, however, in that its roots come
from a blending of African and French cuisine, making for spicy and flavorful
food that is referred to as *criollo*, or Creole, in countries outside of Haiti.

• • • • • • • • • • • • • • • • • •   YIELD: ABOUT 20 FRITTERS   • • • • • • • • • • • • • • • • • •

- 1 quart (946 ml) vegetable oil, such as canola
- 2½ cups (385 g) corn fresh cut from the cob, or (410 g) frozen and thawed
- 1 cup (225 g) masa harina
- 1½ teaspoons sea salt
- 1 teaspoon baking powder
- 2 teaspoons minced thyme
- 1 teaspoon ground chia seeds mixed with ¼ cup (60 ml) water
- Squeeze of lime juice
- 1 cup (235 ml) water

Preheat oil to 360°F (182°C) in a deep fryer or deep pan using a thermometer.

In a large bowl, stir together all the ingredients until a thick batter forms, about 1 minute. Drop by the tablespoonful (15 g) into the preheated oil and allow to cook about 3 minutes until deep golden brown. Transfer to a paper towel or paper bag lined–tray to catch any excess oil.

Serve hot with a zesty dip.

RECIPE NOTE

To make an aioli, a simple accompanying dip, combine ⅓ cup (75 g) vegan mayonnaise with 1 tablespoon (15 ml) lime juice and 1 clove grated garlic.

BEANS AND RICE (GALLO PINTO)

This brilliant recipe is the national dish of Costa Rica for a very good reason—it is fantastic! The Salsa Lizano, a slightly sweet sauce with notes of cumin and pepper that is used extensively as a condiment throughout Costa Rica, is the key to making this otherwise simple and oftentimes overused combination into a spectacular side dish. If you cannot locate Salsa Lizano at your local Mexican or Central American grocery, Pickapeppa or vegan Worcestershire sauce is an adequate replacement.

• • • • • • • • • • • • • • • • • • •   YIELD: 6 SERVINGS   • • • • • • • • • • • • • • • • • • •

FOR THE GALLO PINTO:

- **1 tablespoon (15 ml) olive oil for sautéing**
- **1 red pepper, diced**
- **3 cloves garlic, minced**
- **Dash salt**
- **2½ cups (415 g) cooked white rice, cold**
- **2 cups (512 g) black beans with 1½ cups (355 ml) liquid from cooking (see directions for cooking beans below)**
- **5 tablespoons (75 g) Salsa Lizano**
- **1 teaspoon sea salt, or to taste**
- **½ cup (60 g) minced fresh cilantro**

FOR THE BLACK BEANS:

- **⅔ cup (167 g) dry black beans**
- **Water for soaking and cooking**
- **1 tablespoon (3 g) dried seaweed (optional)**

In a large frying pan over medium-high heat, add the oil, red pepper, and garlic along with a dash or two of salt and sauté for 10 minutes, stirring often to ensure nothing burns.

Add the cold rice and sauté for about 2 minutes or until slightly golden brown on the edges. Add the beans and bean liquid, Salsa Lizano, and sea salt and allow to cook for 7 to 10 minutes or until thickened slightly. Place in a small bowl and invert onto a plate to serve. Top with minced cilantro.

HOW TO COOK DRIED BEANS

To easily cook the dried black beans in this recipe, first sort through the beans to remove any damaged beans or debris. Rinse them well. Soak beans in water (about 3 inches [7.5 cm] from top of dried beans) overnight, or at least 8 hours. Next, rinse beans again, place in a large stockpot, and cover with water about ⅔ of the way full, or about 4 inches (10 cm) above the beans. At this point, you can also add in a tablespoon (3 g) of seaweed, such as kombu, to make them easier to digest. Bring beans to a boil over high heat. Once water is boiling, reduce temperature to a constant simmer (about medium heat) and let cook 1½ to 2 hours or until beans are tender. Salt to taste. Reserve bean liquid for use in the Gallo Pinto.

"SEAFOOD" STEW (ENCEBOLLADO)

This stew is usually made with shellfish of various species, so I replaced it with a common plant-based mock fish, hearts of palm. The result is a zesty dish that is so hearty that you won't even miss the meat.

• YIELD: 4 SERVINGS •

- 1 can (20 ounces, or 560 g) hearts of palm, drained and chopped into small bites
- 1 tablespoon (3 g) dulse flakes
- ½ teaspoon sea salt
- Juice of 1 lime
- 1 tablespoon (15 ml) olive oil for sautéing
- 1 green bell pepper, chopped
- 1 yellow onion, diced
- 1 teaspoon crushed red pepper
- 1 tomato, seeds removed and diced
- 2 cloves garlic, minced
- 1 teaspoon additional sea salt
- 1 can (13.5 ounces, or 400 ml) coconut milk
- 1 tablespoon (10 g) superfine brown rice flour mixed with 3 tablespoons (45 ml) water
- ½ cup (8 g) chopped cilantro
- 3 cups (555 g) cooked rice or quinoa, for serving

Place the hearts of palm and dulse flakes in a small bowl. Toss with sea salt and lime juice and cover. Let rest at least 1 hour, up to 3. Drain and set aside.

Once the hearts of palm have marinated, place a large, deep frying pan over medium-high heat and add the olive oil, bell pepper, onion, red pepper, tomato, garlic, and the sea salt. Sauté about 7 minutes or just until peppers become tender.

Add the coconut milk and hearts of palm and cook over medium heat for about 10 to 15 minutes or until the bell peppers are thoroughly cooked. Drizzle in the flour slurry and whisk quickly to combine into sauce. It will thicken immediately. Let cook briefly while stirring constantly.

Toss in the chopped cilantro and serve immediately over cooked rice or quinoa.

RECIPE NOTE

This dish is typically served as breakfast or lunch in Ecuador and eaten alongside popcorn or plantain chips. But don't let that stop you from enjoying it for dinner, or even a snack, as the rich, savory stew is perfectly filling anytime, day or night.

JAMAICAN JERK TOFU

Scotch bonnet peppers are recommended to create the most authentic-tasting jerk, but if you cannot locate them, an equal amount of habaneros will do just as well.

• • • • • • • • • • • • • • • • • YIELD: 4 TO 6 TOFU STEAKS • • • • • • • • • • • • • • •

- ½ cup (120 ml) rum, dark or white
- 2 Scotch bonnet chiles, diced
- 2 cloves garlic, grated
- 1 tablespoon (8 g) grated ginger
- 2 tablespoons (5 g) minced fresh thyme
- 3 tablespoons (42 g) coconut oil
- 1 tablespoon (7 g) ground cinnamon
- 1 teaspoon ground cloves
- 3 teaspoons (6 g) ground allspice
- 1½ teaspoons ground nutmeg
- 2 teaspoons sea salt
- 2 teaspoons red pepper flakes
- 2 scallions, whites and greens finely chopped
- ¼ cup (60 g) brown sugar
- ¼ cup (60 ml) gluten-free soy sauce
- 2 tablespoons (32 g) tomato paste
- 1 tablespoon (15 ml) lime juice
- ½ cup (120 ml) water
- 1 block (13.5 ounces, or 385 g) extra-firm tofu, drained and pressed at least 2 hours

The day before cooking, place all of the ingredients except the tofu in a medium-size bowl. Whisk together to make a marinade. Cut the tofu into 4 to 6 equal sections, arrange them evenly in a shallow dish, and pour the marinade over them, covering them completely. Cover and refrigerate overnight.

The next day, preheat your oven to 350°F (180°C, gas mark 4). Place the tofu on a nonstick baking sheet and pour any remaining marinade on to coat, letting the bits of spices and such rest on top of the individual tofu steaks.

Bake for 1 hour, flipping once halfway through baking time. Scrape off any remaining spice mixture before serving.

SERVING SUGGESTION:

This tofu is the outstanding star in an easy sandwich. Top it with baby greens, tomato, vegan mayo, and sweet relish. Place in between your favorite vegan bread slices for a spicy and satisfying meal on the go.

COCOA ALMOND TRUFFLES (BRIGADEIROS)

Brigadeiros are similar to truffles in texture and flavor,
but they come together much more quickly and easily than a traditional
truffle. The key to this recipe is making your own condensed almond milk,
which I've included a recipe for below. I recommend using unsweetened
store-bought almond milk to make your own condensed milk rather
than using homemade almond milk, as it seems to yield the most
consistent results when condensing the milk.

·   YIELD: 20 CANDIES   ·

FOR THE CONDENSED ALMOND MILK:

3 cups (700 ml) almond milk
1½ cups (300 g) sugar

Combine the ingredients into a 1-quart (946 ml) saucepan and bring to a boil over medium-high heat. Once boiling, reduce to a constant simmer (not too high as to bubble over) and let cook until reduced to 1 cup (235 ml) liquid, about 45 minutes to 1 hour. Stir at least every 5 minutes, to ensure reduction is occurring and the almond milk is not sticking to the bottom of the pan. It should be the consistency of runny caramel when finished reducing.

FOR THE BRIGADEIROS:

**1 cup (235 ml) condensed almond milk,
  recipe at left**
1 cup (80 g) Dutch-processed cocoa powder
Dash sea salt
1 tablespoon (14 g) coconut oil
¼ cup (48 g) chocolate nonpareil sprinkles

TO MAKE THE BRIGADEIROS: Combine the condensed almond milk, cocoa powder, sea salt, and coconut oil in a small saucepan over medium heat. Let the mixture cook until it begins to easily come away from the bottom of the pan when stirred, about 2 to 3 minutes. Remove from heat and let cool just long enough to make it easy to handle. Roll into 1-inch (2.5 cm) balls and then roll into the chocolate nonpareils to coat.

PEPITA BRITTLE

This is the traditional method of making pepita brittle, which is unlike many nut brittles in that you allow the sugar to completely recrystallize while making the candy. Use a good-quality candy thermometer for easy candy making. This recipe has a very glassy sheen and distinctive crunch.

• • • • • • • • • • • • • • • • YIELD: ABOUT 30 PIECES CANDY • • • • • • • • • • • • • • • •

1½ cups (300 g) granulated sugar
¾ cup (175 ml) water
½ teaspoon fine sea salt
½ vanilla bean, scraped
1 cup (140 g) pepitas (pumpkin seeds)

Prepare a baking sheet by covering with a silicone mat or parchment paper.

In a 2.5-quart (2.4 L) saucepan over medium heat, combine the sugar, water, sea salt, and vanilla bean. Using a candy thermometer, bring the mixture to 238°F (114°C), firm ball stage, stirring often with a wooden spoon and washing down the sides of the pan with a silicone brush.

Once the candy mixture reaches the proper temperature, remove from the heat and stir in the pumpkin seeds. Return to the heat and continue to cook until the mixture crystallizes, which should take around 7 minutes. It will get very clumpy and then literally turn into green-tinged sugar. Cook, stirring constantly until the sugar completely remelts. Time it for about 5 minutes after the sugar crystallizes.

Pour onto the prepared baking sheet and spread thin. Work fast because it hardens quickly. Break into small pieces once the candy is completely cool, after about 1 hour.

DRESS IT UP!

This type of brittle lends itself to flavor additions of all kinds. A touch of cinnamon and black pepper along with the rest of the ingredients for a slightly spicy dessert. Or brush melted chocolate onto the top of the brittle right after spreading and let the chocolate harden before breaking the brittle into individual pieces.

PUMPKIN FRITTERS

Much like Chilean-style sopapillas, these fritters are inspired by the classic fritters of Latin American cuisine, which use pumpkin in their base. They are perfect when served with coffee or tea.

• • • • • • • • • • • • • • • • • • YIELD: ABOUT 20 FRITTERS • • • • • • • • • • • • • • • • • •

Vegetable oil for frying

2 cups (490 g) puréed pumpkin

1¼ cups (150 g) gram flour

½ cup (64 g) cornstarch

¾ cup (102 g) sorghum flour

1 teaspoon baking powder

½ teaspoon baking soda

1 teaspoon sea salt

FOR THE BROWN SUGAR SYRUP:

½ cup (115 g) packed brown sugar or (160 g) agave

1 tablespoon (15 ml) orange juice

1 peeled orange slice

Add oil to a deep fryer and preheat to 360°F (182°C). In a large mixing bowl, combine the pumpkin, gram flour, cornstarch, sorghum flour, baking powder, baking soda, and sea salt until a sticky batter forms.

Using an ice cream scoop, drop by 2-tablespoon (28 g) size balls into the heated oil. Let cook 6 minutes, making sure to gently stir so they don't stick.

Drain on paper towels or brown paper bags. Serve with agave or brown sugar syrup.

TO MAKE THE BROWN SUGAR SYRUP: Simply combine the brown sugar, orange juice, and orange slice in a small pan. Warm gently over low heat until the brown sugar is completely dissolved. Let cook 1 minute and then remove the orange slice.

RECIPE NOTE

Although best eaten fresh, if you are not planning on enjoying these right away, store in a paper bag. Reheat fritters at 350°F (180°C, gas mark 4) for 10 to 15 minutes.

STRAWBERRY CRÊPES WITH SPICED COCONUT CREAM

This is a sweet and spicy take on classic fruit-filled crêpes, using one of the most beloved of fruits, the strawberry, which originates in Chile or Peru. The classic method of macerating the fruit in this recipe creates soft, sweet, and supple strawberries, which make a perfect filling for these tender crêpes.

• • • • • • • • • • • • • • • • YIELD: 7 CRÊPES • • • • • • • • • • • • • • • • • • •

FOR THE CRÊPES:

2 tablespoons (28 ml) olive oil

¼ cup (50 g) sugar

½ cup (64 g) cornstarch

½ cup (80 g) superfine brown rice flour

⅓ cup (80 g) silken tofu

1 cup (235 ml) almond milk

Dash sea salt

Dash cinnamon

½ teaspoon vegan margarine (reserve for cooking)

FOR THE STRAWBERRY FILLING:

4 cups (580 g) whole strawberries

2 tablespoons (26 g) sugar

FOR THE SPICED COCONUT CREAM:

1 can (15 ounces, or 440 ml) full-fat coconut milk

½ teaspoon cinnamon

¼ teaspoon white pepper

Whisk together all ingredients for the batter and chill for at least 2 hours, up to overnight.

Slice the strawberries about ¼-inch (6 mm) thick, discarding the tops, and toss with 2 tablespoons (26 g) sugar. Let rest in the refrigerator for about 2 hours or as long as the crêpe batter rests.

Chill the can of coconut milk in the freezer for about 20 minutes. Once a solid layer of cream has formed on top of the can, carefully scoop out and mix with cinnamon and white pepper. Reserve the rest of the coconut milk for another use.

Over medium heat, warm up a large, nonstick crêpe pan or skillet. Drop about ½ teaspoon nondairy margarine into the pan to coat. Add ⅓ cup (80 ml) batter into the hot pan and quickly swirl around to coat the pan with an even circle of batter. Place back onto the heat and let cook about 2 minutes without trying to flip over the crêpe. It should bubble up slightly, and the edges should remove easily from the pan when ready. Gently lift up using a flat but flexible spatula and flip over carefully. Heat the other side for about 1 to 2 more minutes or until golden brown on both sides. Place on a plate and repeat until all crêpes have been cooked.

Fill each crêpe with about ¼ cup (65 g) macerated strawberries and drizzle the tops with spiced coconut cream.

COCONUT PUDDING (TEMBLEQUE)

This creamy and slightly addictive coconut pudding is a classic dessert often eaten in Puerto Rico. The easy and beautiful pudding can be placed in decorative molds, chilled overnight, and then inverted to capture intricate designs, although I love the look of the simple and very efficient large muffin pan, which generally fits 6 servings.

• • • • • • • • • • • • • • •   YIELD: 4 LARGE OR 6 SMALL SERVINGS   • • • • • • • • • • • • • • •

- **2 cans (13.5 ounces, or 400 ml each) coconut milk**
- **2 cups (475 ml) water**
- **2 cups (400 g) sugar**
- **1 cup (128 g) cornstarch mixed with ½ cup (120 ml) water**
- **1 teaspoon sea salt**
- **1 teaspoon vanilla extract**
- **1 tablespoon (15 g) equal amounts ground cloves, nutmeg, and cinnamon, mixed**

Prepare 4 to 6 molds (large muffin tins work well) by very lightly greasing them with coconut oil or nondairy margarine.

In a 2-quart (2 L) saucepan, combine the coconut milk, water, and sugar and cook over a little higher than medium heat for about 5 minutes, or until the mixture is hot. Add the cornstarch mixture, sea salt, and vanilla extract and, stirring constantly with a whisk over medium heat, let the mixture thicken. It will be done when your wrist begins to hurt, about 7 minutes.

Pour the mixtures into the prepared molds, or serving dishes, and chill overnight. Invert onto a serving tray and dust with a mix of cloves, nutmeg, and cinnamon.

RECIPE NOTE

The name *tembleque* in English translates to "trembling." This perfectly describes the trembling look of the pudding once it has been unmolded and the plate holding the tembleque happens to get bumped gently.

RUM PLANTAIN CAKE

This cake is a lot like a baked sticky pudding
(think date or fig pudding) with an irresistible outer crust
and notes of rum and sweetly ripened plantain.

••••••••••••••••••••••• YIELD: 12 SERVINGS •••••••••••••••••••••••

1 cup (225 g) packed brown sugar

3 very ripe (blackened) plantains

⅓ cup (80 ml) melted coconut oil or olive oil

1½ teaspoons vanilla extract

½ cup (120 ml) dark rum

1 cup (127 g) sorghum flour

½ cup (80 g) superfine brown rice flour

⅓ cup (68 g) sweet white rice flour

1½ teaspoons xanthan gum

3 teaspoons (14 g) baking powder

1 teaspoon sea salt

1 cup (235 ml) + 2 tablespoons (28 ml) almond milk

3 tablespoons (45 ml) lime juice

Preheat the oven to 350°F (180°C, gas mark 4) and lightly grease and flour a standard-size tube pan.

In a large bowl, mash together the brown sugar, plantains, and melted coconut oil or olive oil. Stir in the vanilla extract and dark rum.

In a small separate bowl, whisk together the flours, xanthan gum, baking powder, and sea salt. Slowly add the flour mix into the plantains, alternating with the almond milk, adding a little at a time until all is well mixed. Once all the milk and flour have been added, stir in the lime juice.

Pour the batter into the prepared tube pan and bake for about 1 hour and 25 minutes. The middle will be soft, but the outside crust will be thick and chewy. Let cool completely before serving and store in the refrigerator.

RECIPE NOTE

Give this cake an extra boozy kick and top with an easy banana-rum syrup. Simply purée 1 frozen banana in a blender along with ¼ cup (60 ml) rum, 1 cup (120 g) confectioners' sugar, and just enough water to thin. Pour over the cake just before serving.

CHILEAN-STYLE SWEET GINGER CAKE

This spongy and irresistible cake is studded with crystallized ginger and raisins which make for a very sweet and sophisticated treat. I used the traditional Chilean ginger-flavored cake, *pan de pascua*, as a starting point for my inspiration when developing this recipe.

YIELD: 1 STANDARD BUNDT CAKE OR 6 LARGE MUFFIN-SIZE CAKES

⅔ cup (150 g) vegan margarine

¾ cup (150 g) sugar

1 teaspoon vanilla extract

2 to 3 teaspoons (3 to 8 g) fresh grated ginger

⅓ cup (30 g) tapioca flour

½ teaspoon fine sea salt

1 teaspoon xanthan gum

3 teaspoons (14 g) baking powder

2 cups (240 g) gram flour

¼ cup (80 ml) agave

1½ cups (355 ml) almond milk

½ cup (48 g) crystallized ginger

½ cup (75 g) raisins

Preheat your oven to 350°F (180°C, gas mark 4) and lightly grease and (gram) flour a medium-size metal tube (Bundt) pan or six large muffin-size tins.

In a large mixing bowl, cream together the margarine, sugar, and vanilla extract until smooth. Add the grated ginger, tapioca flour, sea salt, xanthan gum, and baking powder. Add the gram flour, agave, and almond milk and mix vigorously until smooth, about 2 minutes. Fold in the crystallized ginger and raisins until well mixed.

Spoon the batter into the prepared cake pan and bake for 50 minutes or until golden brown on the top and a knife inserted into the middle of the cake comes out clean. Let cool completely before even attempting to remove from the pan. Loosen gently with a butter knife and then invert to remove from the pan.

RECIPE NOTE

Even though the recipe I was inspired by to create this cake comes from Chile, the original origins of *pan de pascua* are German! German immigrants originally introduced the cake to Chile as a variation of stollen—just more evidence that many regional foods are really a combination of different tastes from cultures all over the globe.

MANGO RUM ICE CREAM

This delicious tropical ice cream tastes a lot like a piña colada, without the pineapple, and instead featuring the tangy sweetness of mango. Because it uses alcohol, this is an adult-only indulgence. For a festive addition to parties, serve this ice cream in a frosty mug filled with cream soda or ginger ale.

● ● ● ● ● ● ● ● ● ● ● ● ● ● ● ●   YIELD: 1 QUART (1 L) ICE CREAM   ● ● ● ● ● ● ● ● ● ● ● ● ● ● ● ●

2 large mangoes, peeled and pitted

¼ cup (60 ml) rum, dark or light

½ cup (100 g) sugar

2 cans (13.5 ounces, or 400 ml each) full-fat coconut milk

Dash sea salt

Blend all ingredients until smooth in a food processor or blender and then place the mixture in an ice cream maker. Process the mixture according to manufacturer's instructions. Store in a flexible, airtight container overnight before serving.

RECIPE NOTE

For an extra layer of island flavor, add ¼ cup (24 g) finely chopped candied ginger once the ice cream has been processed by simply stirring it in and allowing it to freeze overnight.

Chapter 5

FABULOUS, FRAGRANT ASIAN AND OCEANIC FARE

Asian cuisine covers a vast area of the globe, including the Middle East, South Asia, Southeast Asia, and Central Asia.

Asian cuisine is probably most notably identified by its abundant variety of spices, which come mainly from India and Indonesia, but have traveled far and wide and become staples all over the globe. Some of these include ginger, tamarind, turmeric, black pepper, cloves, cardamom, basil, and saffron. Even though the cuisines within this large region are very distinct from one area to the next, such as Korean food and Indian food, two things that connect them are the well-placed use of spices and flavorings and the inclusion of a wide variety of fruits and vegetables in various dishes. From the fragrant and filling pomegranate soup of Pakistan to the somewhat spicy staple of Korea called *bulgogi*, if you appreciate spices, this chapter is for you.

Indigenous Oceanic cuisine emerged around 40,000 years ago, when a hunter-gatherer diet developed based on native plants and flora known as "bush foods," such as finger limes and macadamia nuts. This diet continued up until just recently when globalization introduced many Western and Asian dishes to Australia and New Zealand. There is also a lot of British influence in the typical daily meals of an Aussie. Like Australian cuisine, New Zealand food is also heavily British with tropical and Mediterranean notes strewn throughout.

POMEGRANATE SOUP

This Persian soup usually contains meatballs, which I've included
a recipe for below, but it's so hearty on its own it's
really just an extra bit of oomph to include them.

· · · · · · · · · · · · · · · · · · YIELD: 10 OR MORE SERVINGS · · · · · · · · · · · · · · · · · ·

FOR THE SOUP:

1 onion, sliced very thin

2 cloves garlic, minced

1 tablespoon (15 ml) olive oil for sautéing

3¼ teaspoons (16 g) sea salt, divided

¾ cup (169 g) yellow split peas

8 cups (2 L) water

1 teaspoon black pepper

1 teaspoon turmeric

1 small beet, peeled and diced

2 cups (475 ml) pomegranate juice

½ cup each chopped fresh (30 g) parsley, (48 g) mint, and (8 g) cilantro

1 cup (186 g) cooked rice

FOR THE MEATBALLS:

2 cups (80 g) Butler Soy Curls

2 cups (475 ml) salted vegetable broth, warmed until just before boiling

1 teaspoon psyllium husk powder

1 cup (240 g) cooked chickpeas

½ cup (93 g) cooked sushi rice

1 tablespoon (12 g) ground chia seeds mixed with ¼ cup (60 ml) water

½ teaspoon sea salt

2 tablespoons (28 ml) olive oil for brushing

In a large soup pot, sauté the onion, garlic, and olive oil along
with 1 teaspoon sea salt over medium-high heat until translucent,
about 10 minutes. Add the split peas and sauté an additional 1 to
2 minutes, or until golden brown. Add the water, 1½ teaspoons
of the salt, black pepper, turmeric, and beet and bring to a boil.
Once boiling, reduce slightly to simmer. Allow to cook until the
split peas are softened, about 45 minutes to 1 hour.

Stir in the pomegranate juice, the remaining 1¾ teaspoons
salt, herbs, and rice and cook an additional 10 to 15 minutes.

RECIPE NOTE

To make the meatballs, preheat the oven to 350°F (180°C, gas
mark 4). Rehydrate the Soy Curls in the hot vegetable broth for
about 10 minutes or until softened. Drain well and press out any
excess liquid.

Transfer the Soy Curls, psyllium husk, and chickpeas to a food
processor and pulse just until ground. Transfer to a bowl, add the
rice, ground chia gel, and sea salt and use clean hands to knead
into a sticky dough. Roll into small patties, brush each with olive
oil on all sides, and place on an ungreased baking sheet or baking
pan. Bake for about 45 minutes or until dark golden brown and
crispy. Place 2 meatballs in the soup before serving.

TOFU NOODLE SOUP (PHO)

My love for pho, a popular Vietnamese noodle soup often enjoyed
as street food, is undying. I adore the kick of sambal oelek,
a spicy sauce made with chiles and garlic. For me,
the combination of the two is out of this world.

• • • • • • • • • • • • • • • • •   YIELD: 2 VERY LARGE BOWLS OF SOUP   • • • • • • • • • • • • • • • •

6 cups (1.4 L) vegetable broth

2 cloves garlic, minced

1 white onion, sliced very thin

2 carrots, peeled and sliced into long disks

10 broccoli florets

1 teaspoon black pepper

1 teaspoon fresh grated ginger

1 teaspoon ground cinnamon

2 star anise pods

2 to 3 heaping tablespoons (depending on spice preference) (28 to 45 g) sambal oelek

2 tablespoons (28 ml) gluten-free soy sauce or to taste

1 teaspoon salt

8 ounces (225 g) thin rice noodles

2 teaspoons gluten-free soy sauce, or to taste

1 block tofu (12 ounces, or 340 g), drained and pressed well for at least 3 hours

Juice of 1 lime

1 cup (24 g) fresh Thai basil leaves

In a large soup pot over medium-high heat, combine all the ingredients through the tofu and bring to a boil. Simmer gently, just until the broccoli is bright green and slightly tender, about 3 to 5 minutes. Do not overcook!

In a separate pot, cook the rice noodles according to the package directions and rinse very well in cold water to remove starch. Toss with the soy sauce and then divide between 2 deep bowls.

Cut the tofu into about 20 even squares. In each bowl, pour the broth and vegetables on top of the rice noodles and top with the tofu, lime juice, and basil leaves. Serve immediately with a spoon and chopsticks.

COCONUT TOM YUM SOUP

This sweet and sour Thai soup is a wonderful starter and also great as a light lunch or dinner. This recipe freezes especially well, so if you have any extra after making it, freeze it in individual-size freezer-safe containers and just thaw to enjoy a quick and delicious meal!

YIELD: 10 SERVINGS

3 tomatoes, cut into small wedges

2 cloves garlic, minced

2 carrots, cut into thin spears

4 ounces (115 g) shiitake mushroom caps, sliced

2 teaspoons vegetable broth powder or 2 cubes vegetable broth

3 to 6 whole Thai bird chiles

Juice of 2 limes plus the zest

2 coins fresh galangal

½ tablespoon finely minced lemongrass

4 kafir lime leaves, stems removed and halved (dried also works well)

6 cups (1.4 L) water

2 to 3 teaspoons (10 to 15 g) sea salt, or to taste

3 tablespoons (39 g) sugar

1 cup (235 ml) coconut milk

Bring all ingredients except for the coconut milk to a boil in a large soup pot. Once boiling, reduce to a simmer and let cook at least 25 minutes or until the soup is fragrant and the mushrooms are very tender. Stir in the coconut milk and serve hot. Be sure not to eat the kafir lime leaves or galangal. Remove from the soup just before eating.

RECIPE NOTE

Tom Yum Soup is also popular in the neighboring countries of Indonesia, Malaysia, and Singapore; although the name refers to a variety of spicy soups throughout the region.

MINTED GREEN SALAD WITH ORANGES, LENTILS, AND TOMATOES

I fell in love with this salad after only one bite. The earthy undertone and chewiness of the lentils pairs naturally with the robust flavors of the Middle East with the addition of fresh parsley mint.

• YIELD: 4 SERVINGS •

1 ½ cups (297 g) cooked green lentils

1 teaspoon cumin

1 teaspoon sea salt

1 tomato, diced

2 seedless oranges, supremed and chopped (see Recipe Note)

¼ cup (24 g) finely chopped mint

½ cup (30 g) finely chopped parsley

Combine the cooked lentils with the cumin and sea salt. Toss with the tomato, oranges, mint, and parsley. Chill for at least 1 hour before serving.

RECIPE NOTE

To supreme an orange, cut off both the top and bottom of the peel so that you can see the flesh underneath the pith. Use a knife to peel the orange, removing the peel and pith so that only the orange flesh remains. Cut in half and remove the rest of the pith, or white fibers, that remain in the orange, so that the orange divides easily into wedges. Cut into bite-size pieces.

SHREDDED KOHLRABI, PISTACHIO, AND RAISIN SALAD

If you've never eaten shredded kohlrabi before in a salad, this is a great starter recipe. Kohlrabi, a member of the turnip family, has a mild flavor and crunchy texture that make it the perfect complement to the salty, sour, and sweet flavors of the combined ingredients.

• YIELD: 4 SERVINGS •

2 small kohlrabi, peeled and shredded

I carrot, peeled and shredded

I shallot, sliced thin

I tablespoon (2.4 g) thyme leaves

3 scallions, sliced into small rings

½ cup (30 g) loosely packed parsley leaves, minced

I cup (145 g) raisins

Juice of I lemon, about I tablespoon (15 ml)

I teaspoon sea salt (Himalayan recommended)

2 tablespoons (28 g) vegan mayonnaise, such as Vegenaise

Dash or two nutmeg

½ tablespoon agave

Gently mix all ingredients together in a bowl until well mixed. Let flavors meld for about 1 hour and then serve chilled or at room temperature.

RECIPE NOTE

If you are fortunate enough to have kohlrabi growing in your garden, or happen upon one with the leaves still intact, don't toss them. The leaves are delicious and can be served just as you would collard greens or kale.

FALAFEL CUCUMBER SALAD WITH BABA GHANOUSH

My favorite way to enjoy falafel is with a cucumber salad.
(Toss 3 small diced tomatoes, 2 diced cucumbers, 1 minced scallion,
½ cup each of minced [30 g] parsley and [48 g] mint with 1 tablespoon [15 ml]
olive oil, 1 teaspoon salt, and the juice of one lemon.) Top with the
accompanying recipe for baba ghanoush. No pita required.

•   YIELD: 15 FALAFELS   •

FOR THE FALAFEL:

3 cloves roasted garlic

4 cups (960 g) cooked chickpeas

1 cup (160 g) finely minced onion

2 teaspoons ground cumin

1 teaspoon salt

2 teaspoons baking powder

2 cups (240 g) + extra chickpea flour

½ cup (30 g) chopped fresh parsley

½ cup (8 g) chopped fresh cilantro

In a food processor, combine the garlic, chickpeas, onion, cumin, salt, and baking powder and pulse until mixed, scraping down the sides, until thick and smooth, adding a small amount of water if needed.

Transfer the mixture into a large bowl and stir in the chickpea flour. Fold in the parsley and cilantro.

Chill the mixture in the freezer for 15 minutes.

Preheat the oil in a deep fryer to 360°F (185°C).

Form the falafel mixture into fifteen 2 x 1-inch (5 x 2.5 cm) patties. Use a little extra chickpea flour to shape them if they are sticky, but try not to "coat" the patties in it.

Cook the falafel for about 8 minutes in your deep fryer. Transfer to an absorbent paper bag, paper towel, or cloth and serve.

FOR THE BABA GHANOUSH:

3 large eggplants

Salt, to taste

1 tablespoon (15 ml) olive oil

4 cloves garlic

½ cup (120 g) tahini

1 tablespoon (15 ml) lemon juice to thin

1 teaspoon sea salt

Preheat your oven to 400°F (200°C, gas mark 6). Slice the eggplants in half lengthwise and rub the interior flesh lightly with salt. Drizzle with olive oil and then place on a baking sheet, cut side down. Wrap the garlic cloves loosely in foil and roast along with the eggplants. Bake for 1 hour or until the eggplants have become very tender. Once they are roasted, remove the garlic and then broil the eggplants for 5 minutes to add a smoky richness to the baba ghanoush.

Scoop out the roasted eggplant flesh, seeds and all, and place in a food processor along with the roasted garlic, tahini, lemon juice, and sea salt. Process until smooth. Serve hot or at room temperature.

SAVORY STUFFED GRAPES

These little morsels aren't only delicious as finger food, they make an outstanding topping for salads and even sandwiches. Try mixing them into your favorite bed of greens along with a little hummus and a shredded carrot for a complex yet carefree salad.

•••••• YIELD: 10 APPETIZERS ••••••

FOR THE FILLING:

1 cup (240 g) cooked chickpeas
1 teaspoon turmeric
½ teaspoon ground coriander
½ teaspoon nutmeg
1 tablespoon (4 g) minced dill
½ teaspoon sea salt
2 tablespoons (30 ml) tahini
¼ cup (60 ml) water, or to smooth
10 very large globe grapes

Place all the ingredients except the globe grapes in a food processor and pulse until very smooth, scraping the sides as necessary.

Slice off the tops of the grapes and set aside. Using a small measuring spoon, such as a ¼ teaspoon, evenly scoop out the middles and seeds so that only the shell of the grape remains (this can also be done easily with cherry tomatoes). Use a piping bag to pipe the filling to the grapes and replace the tops. Chill before serving.

MASALA MUSHROOM CAPS

This recipe makes a fun appetizer or finger food for parties and comes together easily, so it's a snap to prepare right before guests arrive. The kalonji seeds have a bitter, pungent taste and a striking black color that adds a fun touch to this dish. They can easily be sourced from Indian markets along with the other spices and gram flour.

•••••• YIELD: 30 APPETIZERS ••••••

30 large cremini or button mushroom caps
2 teaspoons olive oil
½ cup (80 g) minced yellow onion
1 cup (100 g) finely chopped cauliflower florets
½ teaspoon coriander
½ teaspoon cumin
1½ teaspoons fine sea salt
Dash asafetida
1 teaspoon garam masala
⅛ teaspoon cardamom
¾ cup (90 g) gram flour mixed with ½ cup (120 ml) water
Kalonji seeds, to garnish

Preheat your oven to 385°F (195°C).

Clean out the caps of the mushrooms so that they can easily be stuffed. Place upside down on a small baking sheet and drizzle lightly with olive oil. In a medium-size bowl, combine the onion, cauliflower, coriander, cumin, sea salt, asafetida, garam masala, cardamom, and gram flour mixed with water. Stir well to combine and fill the mushroom caps with the mixture, piling high. Top with kalonji seeds to garnish and bake for 25 minutes. Serve slightly cooler than hot.

VIETNAMESE SALAD WRAPS

These easy salad wraps are a traditional starter for a
Vietnamese meal. They are a lot like spring rolls, but instead of
being filled with cooked vegetables and deep-fried, they are eaten
uncooked and generally feature rice noodles, tofu, and fresh raw vegetables.
In these salad wraps, I replaced the rice noodles with raw zucchini
and carrot "noodles" for an extra dose of delicious veggies.

•   YIELD: 12 SALAD WRAPS   •

FOR THE SALAD WRAPS:

- **1 zucchini, julienned**
- **2 carrots, julienned**
- **1 tablespoon (15 ml) gluten-free soy sauce**
- **1 teaspoon frozen grated lemongrass**
- **12 rice paper wraps**
- **1 block (8 ounces, or 220 g), smoked tofu, sliced into ½-inch (1 cm) wide x 2-inch (5 cm) long strips**
- **30 fresh Thai basil leaves**

FOR THE SAUCE:

- **4 tablespoons (60 ml) gluten-free soy sauce**
- **2 tablespoons (28 ml) mirin**
- **1½ teaspoons Chinese five-spice powder**
- **2 heaping tablespoons (32 g) creamy peanut butter**
- **2 tablespoons (28 g) red bean paste (anko)**
- **1 tablespoon (9 g) crushed peanuts, for garnish**

TO MAKE THE SALAD WRAPS: In a medium-size bowl, toss the zucchini, carrots, soy sauce, and lemongrass together until well mixed. Run 1 sheet rice paper wrap under water just briefly to get entirely wet (it will soften more once removed from the water stream) and place on a clean, flat surface. In the middle of the circular paper, place about ¼ cup (55 g) julienned carrot and zucchini mixture, then 1 strip tofu, and a few basil leaves and then wrap up: first the bottom, then the sides, and finally, close over the top and press down to seal. The papers will get very sticky if you wait too long to roll them, so work quickly when wrapping and wet only 1 paper at a time. Repeat until all papers are used.

TO MAKE THE DIPPING SAUCE: Simply whisk all the ingredients together, except the peanuts, and then top with the crushed peanuts to garnish.

RECIPE NOTE

Rice paper wraps are easy to locate in Asian grocery stores. They are typically stocked alongside the rice noodles or nori sheets.

INDIAN POTATO FRITTERS (BATATA VADA)

There are few things I love more than a potato-based Indian appetizer. When I had to go gluten-free, I was devastated at my loss of being able to enjoy a true-blue samosa ever again, but I think these more than make up for it. The entire fritter is made up of ingredients similar to a samosa, minus the pastry.

• YIELD: ABOUT 18 FRITTERS •

Vegetable oil for deep fryer

3 large shallots

1 teaspoon mustard seed

1 teaspoon cumin seed

1 teaspoon asafetida

2½ teaspoons sea salt, divided

1 teaspoon olive oil

3 medium yellow potatoes, boiled whole until fork tender

1 cup (130 g) frozen peas, thawed

1 cup (110 g) gram flour

1 cup (235 ml) water

Pinch additional sea salt

Preheat the oil for a deep fryer to 360°F (182°C).

In a medium-size frying pan, sauté the shallots, mustard seed, cumin seed, asafetida, 1 teaspoon sea salt, and 1 teaspoon olive oil over medium-high heat until the shallots are golden brown on the edges, about 10 minutes. Take off the heat.

In a medium-size bowl, mash the boiled potatoes, leaving a few big lumps remaining throughout. Stir in the sautéed shallot mixture, peas, and 1 teaspoon sea salt.

In a separate bowl, whisk together the gram flour, water, and ½ teaspoon sea salt until smooth. Roll the mashed potatoes into 18 golf-ball-size balls and then dip into the gram flour batter, letting any excess drip back into the bowl. Fry about 3 at a time for 10 minutes. Transfer to a paper towel or paper bag–lined metal tray to absorb any excess oil. Serve with chutney (recipe below).

DATE CHUTNEY:

Make an easy accompaniment to the fritters by puréeing 10 dried dates with ½ cup (120 ml) water until smooth. Place in a small pan and add 1 tablespoon (15 ml) vinegar, 1 tablespoon (13 g) sugar, 1 teaspoon salt, and a dash each of cardamom and cinnamon. Cook over medium heat, stirring often, until thickened (about 5 minutes). Cool completely.

"BACON 'N' EGG," PINEAPPLE BEETROOT BURGER

In Australia, this assortment of toppings is standard for enjoying a burger. As skeptical as I was when I first learned about this combination, it is now one of my favorite ways to enjoy a veggie burger. For best results, prepare everything separately and assemble right before eating.

YIELD: 12 BURGERS, 12 EGGS

FOR THE BURGERS:

- 1½ cups (257 g) cooked pinto beans
- 1 cup (96 g) textured vegetable protein (TVP) rehydrated in 1 cup (235 ml) vegetable broth for 10 minutes
- 2 cloves garlic, grated
- 1 carrot, grated
- 1 small beet, peeled and grated
- ½ teaspoon sea salt
- ½ cup (60 g) gluten-free bread crumbs

Preheat your oven to 375°F (190°C, gas mark 5).

In a large bowl, smash together the pinto beans and prepared TVP using a potato masher until very well combined. Blend in the rest of the ingredients using a large fork (or clean hands) to make a homogenous mixture.

Brush a large baking pan with oil, and then shape the mixture into about 12 patties and place on the pan. Brush the tops of the patties with a little more oil and bake for 45 to 60 minutes, flipping once halfway through.

FOR THE "EGGS":

- 1 block tofu (14 ounces, or 397 g), extra firm, drained and pressed slightly
- 2 teaspoons black salt
- ½ cup (60 g) gram flour mixed with ½ cup (120 ml) water

Use a fork to mix together all the ingredients in a small bowl. Coat a medium-size frying pan with a little oil, heat over medium high, and drop ¼ cup (55 g) "egg" onto pan. Allow it to cook about 3 minutes, flip, and repeat. Be sure to let the patty cook through completely, about 6 minutes total.

FOR THE ASSEMBLED BURGER:

- 12 gluten-free hamburger buns
- ½ cup (115 g) vegan mayonnaise
- 1½ cups (30 g) arugula leaves
- 12 slices canned pineapple, drained
- 12 burgers
- 1 large avocado, sliced into 24 thin pieces
- 24 pieces "bacon" (Smokey Tempeh, "Bacon" recipe, page 158)
- 12 "eggs"
- 2 medium-size tomatoes, sliced into about 12 slices
- 12 slices pickled beetroot, drained

TO ASSEMBLE: Lightly toast gluten-free buns (Schärs brand is great!) and spread a touch of vegan mayonnaise on the insides of each half of the bun. Assemble, from bottom up: bottom bun, arugula, pineapple, burger, avocado, "bacon," "egg," tomato, beetroot slice, top bun. Eat unabashedly, but a napkin is quite helpful.

SPINACH MUSHROOM CURRY (SAAG MUSHROOM)

I call this one a fusion recipe because although it resembles typical saag mushroom in taste and appearance, it's quite different from the authentic version. Featuring butternut squash as a stand-in for heavy cream, this lightened-up version will still satisfy your craving for tasty North Indian cuisine.

•   YIELD: 4 SERVINGS   •

2 tablespoons (28 ml) olive oil

8 curry leaves

1 large Vidalia onion, diced

2 cloves garlic, minced

2 coins fresh ginger, minced

10 ounces (280 g) white button mushrooms, sliced

1 teaspoon sea salt

1 butternut squash, roasted (see recipe note below) and mashed

½ tablespoon olive oil

11 ounces (310 g) baby spinach leaves

Sea salt, to taste

In a large frying pan, heat the olive oil over medium-high heat and add the curry leaves, onion, garlic, ginger, mushrooms, and sea salt. Sauté until the onions and mushrooms begin to caramelize and turn a rich golden brown, about 15 minutes. Stir the mashed roasted squash into the mushrooms. Let simmer over very low heat for about 10 minutes.

Add the olive oil to a separate frying pan over medium heat and cook the spinach and sea salt just until wilted. I like to cook half, then add fresh leaves to the top, and flip over the cooked leaves to weigh down the fresh leaves, about 5 minutes total cooking time. Drain the excess water and then transfer to a food processor. Pulse briefly until well chopped but not puréed. Combine with the mushrooms and squash mixture and serve hot over basmati rice.

RECIPE NOTE

To easily roast the butternut squash, cut in half lengthwise and scoop out the seeds. Peel using a vegetable peeler and cut the squash into 1-inch (2.5 cm) wide cubes.

Place the cubed squash on a parchment-covered baking sheet, lightly drizzle with olive oil, and sprinkle with sea salt. Bake in a preheated oven at 400°F (200°C, gas mark 6) for about 30 minutes or until fork tender. Flip the cubes halfway through cooking time.

INDIAN CRÊPES WITH SORREL AND SPINACH (BESAN CHEELA)

These crêpes are unlike traditional French crêpes in that they are thicker and a little firmer. Feel free to fill them with whatever you fancy if sorrel and spinach don't do it for you. Sautéed mushrooms and garlic are also a fantastic choice.

YIELD: ABOUT 5 CRÊPES

¼ cup (36 g) minced mild green chile pepper, such as poblano or Anaheim

3 shallots, minced

½ cup (8 g) chopped cilantro

1 teaspoon ajwain seeds

Pinch turmeric

½ teaspoon baking powder

1¾ cups (210 g) + 2 tablespoons (15 g) gram flour

1 teaspoon sea salt

1¼ tablespoons (19 ml) olive oil

1½ cups (355 ml) water

1 cup (30 g) finely chopped spinach leaves

¼ cup (8 g) finely chopped sorrel

½ teaspoon sea salt

½ teaspoon olive or coconut oil

Combine all the ingredients through the 1 teaspoon sea salt in a large bowl and mix well. Stir in the olive oil and water to form a medium-bodied batter.

In a small bowl, toss together the spinach, sorrel, and salt. Set aside.

Heat a large nonstick pan on a little higher than medium heat and coat the bottom of the pan with about ½ teaspoon oil. Add ½ cup (139 g) batter and quickly move the pan in a circular motion to spread the batter into a crêpe. Let cook, about 1 to 2 minutes, until bubbles have formed on the crêpe and the top of the crêpe no longer has much visibly wet batter. Sprinkle on about 2 tablespoons (4 g) chopped spinach and sorrel. Flip over half of the crêpe to cover the chopped spinach and press down gently with a spatula, as you would cook a filled omelet. Flip over and cook an additional 1 minute or until both sides turn golden brown. Repeat with the remaining batter, adding ½ cup (139 g) at a time.

Serve with your favorite chutney or plain coconut yogurt and fresh chopped cilantro.

AUSTRALIAN VEGGIE PIE

Australia's native dish is what's known as meat pie,
a small personal-size pie with a flaky crust that's filled with meat.
This version is family-sized (although it can easily be made into mini pies),
uses a variety of veggies instead of beef, and is no less satisfying.

· · · · · · · · · · · · · · · · · YIELD: 1 STANDARD-SIZE VEGGIE PIE, · · · · · · · · · · · · · · · ·
ABOUT 12 SERVINGS

FOR THE FILLING:

- **1 tablespoon (15 ml) olive oil**
- **1 cup (164 g) cooked corn**
- **½ red onion, diced**
- **2 carrots, chopped into small pieces**
- **1 clove garlic, minced**
- **1 red potato, diced**
- **2 teaspoons sea salt, divided**
- **1 stalk celery, diced**
- **1 tablespoon (2.5 g) fresh minced sage**
- **1 cup (100 g) green beans**
- **1 cup (160 g) cooked green peas**
- **1 teaspoon sea salt**
- **1 tablespoon (12 g) ground chia seeds mixed with ¼ cup (60 ml) water**
- **3 tablespoons (42 g) vegan margarine, softened**
- **¼ cup (40 g) superfine brown rice flour**

FOR THE CRUST:

- **1 recipe pastry crust from Baked Pierogi (page 76)**

Preheat your oven to 350°F (180°C, gas mark 4).

TO MAKE THE FILLING: In a large frying pan, heat the olive oil over medium-high heat. Add the corn, onion, carrots, garlic, potato, and celery and sauté just until slightly tender, about 10 minutes. Lightly salt with 1 teaspoon of the sea salt while cooking. Mix the rest of the ingredients into the sautéed veggies and then set aside.

TO MAKE THE CRUST: Prepare the crust from Baked Pierogi, page 76, divide into 2 even sections, and roll each out between 2 sheets of plastic wrap until ¼-inch (6 mm) thick. Gently transfer one section of the rolled dough to the bottom of a standard-size deep-dish greased pie pan and press down the edges using a fork or your fingers. Poke a few holes in the crust using a fork.

Transfer the filling on top of the bottom crust to fill the pie pan. Top the pie with the second piece of rolled-out dough and seal by pinching it together. Cut a few small slits in the top of the crust and bake for 30 minutes. Increase the oven temperature to 400°F (200°C, gas mark 6) and bake an additional 20 to 25 minutes. Let cool about 20 minutes before serving.

Serve with ketchup for an authentically Aussie-style main course.

NIGIRI AND MAKI SUSHI

Sushi comes in many different forms; the following recipes highlight two of the most popular ways to enjoy the dishes . . . minus the fishes. Serve them together for a fun sushi dinner sampler or just make one for a satisfying main course in an Asian-inspired meal.

• • • • • • • • • • YIELD: 8 NIGIRI SUSHI, 24 PIECES MAKI SUSHI • • • • • • • • • • •

FOR THE NIGIRI:

2 cups (372 g) cooked sushi rice

1 tablespoon (15 ml) sushi vinegar

½ papaya, sliced extra thin, seeds reserved

1 sheet nori, cut into strips ¼-inch (6 mm) wide

2 tablespoons (18 g) papaya seeds

Mix the rice and vinegar and shape into 2-inch (5 cm) logs using slightly wet hands. Cut the papaya into 2 x 1-inch (5 x 2.5 cm) rectangles. Place 1 nori strip down on a flat surface with 1 rice log placed perpendicular on top of the nori. Put the cut papaya on top of the sushi logs, fold up the nori strip tightly, and use a touch of water to seal into place like a piece of tape. Top with papaya seeds. Serve with wasabi, pickled ginger, and gluten-free soy sauce or tamari.

FOR THE MAKI:

8 sheets nori

1 tablespoon (15 ml) sushi vinegar

2½ cups (465 g) cooked sushi rice

8 spears steamed asparagus

1 small carrot, julienned

1 small cucumber, julienned

1 to 2 avocados, pitted, peeled, and cut into thin spears

15 leaves baby bok choy

Place 1 sheet of nori on a clean and dry flat surface. Have a small bowl of water next to your workspace as well as a sharp knife and easy access to a sink. Mix the vinegar into the sushi rice and smooth out about ⅓ cup (62 g) rice into a flat sheet over the lower ⅓ of the nori wrap.

On top of the rice, layer 1 spear of asparagus, a few sprigs both julienned carrot and cucumber, and 2 spears avocado so that they all remain only in the center of the rice and stretch the entire surface of the nori wrap. Gently wet the very top portion of the roll (the farthest away from the rice and veggies) and then use both hands to roll them up tightly. A sushi mat comes in handy here, but isn't necessary.

Roll up like a cigar, as tight as possible, and then slice, with a very sharp and clean knife, into 1-inch (2.5 cm) coins. Repeat until all sushi wraps have been used. Serve with wasabi, pickled ginger, and gluten-free soy sauce or tamari.

BULGOGI-STYLE TOFU

This recipe was created to satisfy the craving I would occasionally get for bulgogi, a popular dish in Korea made from marinated thin strips of beef that literally translates to "fire meat." As one who regularly enjoyed the classic beef version in my pre-vegan days, I can say that this tofu version does not skip a beat. My favorite brand of tofu to use with this recipe is Twin Oaks brand, which is sold at many natural foods stores and Whole Foods locations. Twin Oaks brand of tofu is dense and firm enough to cut into very thin strips. If you cannot locate this brand, any firm tofu that has been very well pressed (8 or more hours) will work well, too.

•   YIELD: 6 SERVINGS   •

1 block (16-ounces, or 455 g) extra-firm, very dense tofu

4 scallions, chopped (use white parts, too!)

3 cloves garlic, minced

½ average-size onion, sliced

1 heaping teaspoon fresh grated ginger

⅔ cup (160 ml) gluten-free tamari or soy sauce

¼ cup (60 g) toasted sesame oil

6 tablespoons (72 g) organic sugar

1 teaspoon black pepper

1 teaspoon crushed red pepper flakes

¼ cup (60 ml) mirin

2 tablespoons (28 ml) rice vinegar

¼ cup (40 g) shredded pear, skin and all

Sesame oil for frying

First, make sure your tofu is very well drained.

Slice into very thin pieces (as thin as you can without tearing) and arrange in an 8-inch (20 cm) dish, about 2-inches (5 cm) deep. Stack so that the marinade can easily flow through.

Combine all the rest of the ingredients and pour over top of the sliced tofu. Cover with plastic wrap and let rest in the refrigerator overnight or at least 8 hours.

The next day, carefully remove the tofu (it should be light brown by now) from the pan and reserve the marinade.

Heat up a large frying pan over medium-high heat and drizzle generously with sesame oil to coat. Once the pan is hot, add 1 layer of marinated tofu and cook for 10 to 15 minutes. Flip over once the edges of the tofu are browned on one side and then repeat. Remove the tofu and repeat with the rest of the tofu. Once it is all nice and browned on both sides, return all tofu to the pan and simmer in the marinade until most of the liquid is gone, about 10 more minutes.

Serve over sticky rice along with some kimchi.

CHOCOLATE LOLLY CAKE

This is one confection that is almost exclusively eaten in New Zealand. It typically uses malt cookies and "lollies," fruity candies resembling marshmallows that come in a variety of colors and flavors, but the stand-ins I used bring a smile to kids' faces just as easily. This is perfect for adding a little playfulness to a potluck or other friendly gathering.

• • • • • • • • • • • • • •   YIELD: 1 LOLLY CAKE, OR 20 SERVINGS   • • • • • • • • • • • • • • •

4 cups (400 g) crushed (pulsed in food processor) gluten-free animal cookies

2 tablespoons (10 g) dark cocoa powder

½ cup (120 ml) coconut milk

½ cup (112 g) vegan margarine, melted

½ cup (88 g) nondairy chocolate chips

2 cups (175 g) vegan marshmallows, such as Sweet and Sara brand, assorted colors if possible

2 cups (170 g) sweetened shredded coconut

In a large bowl, combine the crushed animal cookies with the dark cocoa powder and blend until smooth. Add the coconut milk, vegan margarine, chocolate chips, and marshmallows and form into a loaf shape. Roll the loaf into the shredded coconut to completely cover. Freeze for 15 minutes or until firm. Transfer to the refrigerator for storage and cut into 1-inch (2.5 cm) thick slices to serve.

Mix it Up!

Try adding different varieties of candies or "lollies" to this cake to add some flare. There are many varieties of vegan candies on the market, and each would bring its own unique qualities to a lolly cake. For instance, mixing a few cut-up chunks of vegan peanut butter cups into this would be awfully delicious, albeit incredibly (but edibly) sweet!

BANANA NEPALESE PANCAKES WITH "BACON"

Traditional Nepalese pancakes, called *malpua*, are made similarly to these, but they are deep-fried. To save a few calories, I made this batter work with light pan frying instead. These pancakes taste truly delightful (albeit more American) served with the accompanying recipe for Smoky Tempeh Bacon.

• • • • • • • • • • • • • YIELD: 12 MINI PANCAKES, 12 STRIPS "BACON" • • • • • • • • • • • •

BANANA NEPALESE PANCAKES:

2 bananas, mashed

1 tablespoon (12 g) ground chia seeds mixed with ¼ cup (60 ml) water

½ cup (100 g) sugar

1½ teaspoons baking powder

1 teaspoon cardamom

¾ teaspoon sea salt

1 teaspoon xanthan gum

½ cup (80 g) superfine brown rice flour

½ cup (60 g) gram flour

2 tablespoons (28 ml) olive oil

½ cup (120 ml) nondairy milk

Combine all the ingredients into a medium-size bowl and whisk until smooth. Heat a nonstick skillet just above medium heat (6 out of 10) and drop about ½ teaspoon margarine or coconut oil onto the pan once hot. Pour approximately ⅛ cup (28 g) of batter onto the pan and let cook for 1½ to 2 minutes before attempting to flip. I can fit about 4 small pancakes onto 1 pan. There should be bubbles on the surface, and it should be easy to flip the cakes over. Flip gently, as they are fragile, and allow to cook about 1 more minute on the opposite side. Serve with sliced bananas on top and your favorite flavor of syrup.

SMOKEY TEMPEH "BACON":

1 package (8 ounces, or 227 g) tempeh

⅓ cup (80 ml) red wine

½ tablespoon liquid smoke

¼ cup (80 g) maple syrup

⅛ cup (28 ml) gluten-free soy sauce

⅓ cup (80 ml) olive oil

1 teaspoon vegetable broth seasoning

Dash allspice

½ teaspoon smoked paprika

Black pepper

½ teaspoon sea salt

Slice the tempeh into 12 long, thin strips and place in a shallow dish, about 9 x 9 inches (23 x 23 cm). Whisk together all of the remaining ingredients in a small bowl and pour over the tempeh strips to cover. Let marinate overnight or at least 8 hours, flipping once halfway through.

Preheat the oven to 300°F (150°C, gas mark 2).

Transfer the marinated strips to a parchment-covered baking sheet and bake for 1 hour to 1 hour 20 minutes, flipping once halfway through until the "bacon" is dark brown in color and crispy.

STRAWBERRY MOCHI CAKE (ICHIGO DAIFUKU)

Daifuku, a traditional Japanese confection made from glutinous sticky rice and usually stuffed with red bean paste, is a popular treat eaten in Japan and can be made in a variety of ways. If you've been to an Asian grocery, chances are good that you've seen these colorful mochi-based treats. Ichigo daifuku is a great type to make at home, as the strawberry filling is very perishable, making them difficult to find at the market.

YIELD: 12 PIECES

1 cup (204 g) mochiko (sweet white rice flour)

1 cup (235 ml) almond milk

1 teaspoon coconut oil

½ teaspoon apple cider vinegar

1 drop food coloring (red makes the ones shown)

Tapioca or potato starch for dusting

½ cup (85 g) sweet red bean paste (anko)

12 small strawberries, greens removed

¼ cup (50 g) sugar

Place all the ingredients through the food coloring in a microwavable bowl and whisk together until smooth. Lightly cover with plastic wrap and microwave on high for 6 minutes.

Let the mixture cool just until you are able to handle it and then dust your hands with potato starch and transfer it in between 2 pieces of plastic wrap. Roll out until about ½ to ¼-inch (1 cm to 6 mm) thick. Use a pizza cutter to cut into even squares, about 2-inches (5 cm) square.

Do the same thing with the bean paste. Coat your hands with tapioca starch, place the paste between 2 pieces of plastic wrap, and roll out until thin, about ½ to ¼-inch (1 cm to 6 mm) thick. Cut into squares and, using starch-covered hands, cover a small strawberry with the bean paste. Then place it in the middle of a square of mochi and gently pull up each corner of the square to cover the strawberry, twisting to seal with each corner until covered. Pat to smooth into an even patty. If at any point it gets too sticky to handle, dust again gently with tapioca starch.

Refrigerate until ready to eat, up to 48 hours.

RECIPE NOTE

Daifuku can easily be made with just the bean paste (rolled into a ball) for a treat that lasts longer and is just as tasty. I also find it fun to experiment with other types of fillings wrapped in the bean paste, such as pitted cherries, frozen bananas (store the daifuku in the freezer once assembled), and blueberries. Add 1 tablespoon (5 g) cocoa powder to the bean paste for a chocolate daifuku. Really, the combinations are endless!

LAMINGTON CAKES

These little beauties caught my eye as I was researching Australian desserts, and I knew I had to veganize and de-glutenize them. The spongy interior matches perfectly with the soft exterior of the chocolate ganache and the chewy contrast of shredded coconut.

•••••••••••••••••••• YIELD: ABOUT 30 CAKES ••••••••••••••••••••

FOR THE CAKE:

- 1 cup (200 g) sugar
- 1 cup (160 g) superfine brown rice flour
- ¼ cup (48 g) potato starch
- ¾ cup (90 g) gram flour
- ¼ cup (51 g) sweet white rice flour
- 1 teaspoon xanthan gum
- 2 teaspoons baking powder
- 1 teaspoon sea salt
- 2 tablespoons (24 g) ground chia seeds mixed with ½ cup (120 ml) water
- 1 cup (235 ml) almond milk, divided
- ¼ cup (56 ml) coconut oil, softened

FOR THE GANACHE:

- 1 cup (235 ml) coconut milk
- 1½ cups (263 g) nondairy chocolate chips
- 2 cups (160 g) shredded coconut

TO MAKE THE CAKE: Preheat the oven to 350°F (180°C, gas mark 4). Line an 8 x 8-inch (20 x 20 cm) pan with a sheet of parchment paper. In a large bowl, whisk together the sugar, brown rice flour, potato starch, gram flour, sweet white rice flour, xanthan gum, baking powder, and sea salt until well blended.

Add ½ the flour mixture to a mixing bowl along with the prepared chia seed mixture, ½ cup (60 ml) almond milk, and coconut oil. Mix well and add in the remaining flour mixture and almond milk. Spread the batter in the prepared cake pan.

Bake for 35 minutes or until spongy to the touch and the color is light golden brown. Let cool completely and then cut into small squares.

TO MAKE THE GANACHE: Simply warm the coconut milk over medium heat for about 5 minutes, just until it plops, but is not boiling. Place chocolate chips in a heat-safe bowl and pour the coconut milk over the chips and stir to melt. Let rest 15 minutes.

TO ASSEMBLE: Dip the cut cakes into the ganache and let harden in the freezer for about 10 minutes, just until firmed up a bit. Roll in the shredded coconut to coat and return to refrigerator to completely harden.

Chapter 6

FROM CANADA TO MEXICO: A NORTH AMERICAN MENU

North American cuisine includes the tip top of the continent in Canada all the way down to Mexico, and nestled in between is the culinary melting pot of the United States. Native Americans invented a number of cooking methods, which have combined with many European cooking techniques to form what we consider American cuisine today.

Canada's cuisine is even more widely varied than that of the United States with culinary influences literally from all over the globe because of the large amount of immigrants from all over the world who have settled there.

Mexico, on the other hand, definitely sticks to its own fiery local cuisine and embellishes its food with beautifully colored native vegetables and plenty of chile peppers for kick.

MINI POTATO SKINS

This classic American sports-bar finger food gets downsized by using fingerlings in place of the common larger potato. What results is a tender, yet crispy, and incredibly irresistible appetizer. I recommend using a vegan cheese that doesn't get too runny, such as Daiya, when melted to retain the desired balance of crispy skins to chewy cheese.

· · · · · · · · · · · · · · · · · ·   YIELD: 20 MINI POTATO SKINS   · · · · · · · · · · · · · · · · · ·

10 fingerling potatoes

FOR THE RUB:
2 tablespoons (28 ml) olive oil
1 tablespoon (6 g) nutritional yeast
1 clove garlic, grated
1 teaspoon sea salt
1 teaspoon smoked paprika
Fresh cracked black pepper

FOR THE TOPPINGS:
1 cup (112 g) Cheddar-style shredded vegan cheese
¼ cup (17 g) shredded kale
½ cup (115 g) vegan sour cream
1 scallion, sliced very thin
¼ cup (20 g) vegan bacon bits

Preheat the oven to 400°F (200°C, gas mark 6). Poke a few holes in the fingerlings using a fork and then bake for 30 minutes until softened and skin is crackly. Remove from the oven to cool and increase the oven temperature to 450°F (230°C, gas mark 8).

Once the fingerlings are cool enough to handle, carefully cut them in half lengthwise and scrape out a good portion of the filling, but leave about ¼ inch's (6 mm) worth of potato still clinging to the skins.

Combine all the ingredients for the "rub," rub onto both sides of the potato skins, and place on a baking sheet. Bake for 5 minutes, flip over (using tongs), and bake an additional 5 minutes.

Remove from the oven, fill with the cheese, and sprinkle with kale and then bake 5 more minutes and top it off with a 2-minute broil. Remove from the oven, plate up, and top with sour cream, scallion, and bacon bits.

QUICK MASHED POTATOES

Don't toss out the extra potato you scraped from the skins. Instead, place it in a bowl and mash along with about 1 teaspoon sea salt, 2 tablespoons (30 g) vegan sour cream, and a sprinkling of nutritional yeast for a simple side. Or transfer to freezer-safe plastic bag and freeze. Use later to thicken soups, sauces, or stews.

STUFFED ZUCCHINI FLOWERS

Even though zucchini flowers are usually battered and fried, I find them most delectable when they're cleaned well and eaten raw. You can really taste the floral notes and the zucchini when enjoyed this way, and the delicacy of each doesn't get crowded out by oil and breading. These also make lovely salad toppers when stuffed and go nicely alongside the mole sauce featured on page 194.

· YIELD: 11 APPETIZERS ·

11 zucchini blossoms
1 cup (230 g) vegan cream cheese
2 teaspoons cumin
⅓ cup (16 g) chopped chives
½ tablespoon nutritional yeast

Wash your zucchini flowers by letting them soak in salty water for about 10 minutes, which ensures no dirt is lurking inside. Remove and gently pat dry.

Mix together the cream cheese, cumin, chives, and nutritional yeast in a small bowl. Place in a piping bag. From the bottom of the flower, not where the orange petals are, but where the sturdy green base is, slice off enough of the green just to create an opening and pipe in the filling until well filled, gently clasping the ends closed so the filling does not come out the other side.

Chill before serving alongside a dipping sauce. One of my favorites is a simple mix of ½ cup (115 g) vegan mayonnaise, 2 teaspoons (6 g) chipotle powder, 1 teaspoon cocoa powder, 1 teaspoon agave, and 1 tablespoon (15 ml) lime juice.

RECIPE NOTE

When sourcing zucchini flowers, choose flowers which have been freshly removed, preferably in the morning, and are still closed as they are less likely to have any bugs inside.

MANGO AND TOMATILLO SALSA

This delicious salsa is a perfect use for tomatillos,
which we always have growing in our summer garden. Rinse the
tomatillos well to remove the sticky substance that coats the
fruit once the paper-lantern-like covering is removed.

•••••••••••••••••••••••••••••• YIELD: 3 CUPS (780 G) SALSA ••••••••••••••••••••••••

9 medium-size tomatillos

1 tablespoon (15 ml) olive oil

**1 bunch cilantro, mostly leaves
(about 1 cup [16 g], unpacked)**

2 cloves garlic

**1 jalapeño, roasted along with
tomatillos (seeded)**

Juice of 1 lime

1 teaspoon coriander

1 teaspoon sea salt

1 large mango, diced

Preheat the oven to 425°F (220°C, gas mark 7). Quarter the
tomatillos and in a small bowl, toss with the olive oil. Place on
a baking sheet and roast for 10 minutes.

When finished, place in a food processor with all the other
ingredients excluding the mango and blend together. Add the
diced mango. Pulse a few times just until blended. Serve with
tortilla chips or as a condiment with your favorite Mexican dish.

Homemade Tortilla Chips

To make quick and easy tortillas chips from corn tortillas, simply
use a pizza cutter to slice into triangles. Lightly brush each side
of the triangles with olive oil, salt lightly, and bake at 400°F
(200°C, gas mark 6) until crisp on both sides, flipping once
halfway through, about 12 minutes total.

PECAN-CRUSTED CHILE RELLENOS

Poblanos are beautiful, deep green, shiny, and slightly piquant peppers that are the stars of the show in chile rellenos. This baked version is not only healthier than the typical version, it's also animal friendly! Try and source a good-quality vegan cheese that is not runny when it melts, but rather stretchy, as it is integral to the texture, and therefore, taste, of a proper chile relleno.

YIELD: 4 SERVINGS

FOR THE PEPPERS:

4 poblano peppers, roasted until skins are easily removed (see note)

1½ cups (168 g) shredded vegan pepper jack-style or other white cheese (Daiya brand works great)

FOR THE BATTER:

¾ cup (90 g) + 2 tablespoons (15 g) gram flour

½ cup (120 ml) water

1 teaspoon sea salt

¼ teaspoon cumin

¼ teaspoon smoked paprika

FOR THE CRUST:

1½ cups (165 g) finely ground pecans

Preheat the oven to 400°F (200°C, gas mark 6). Remove the seeds carefully by splitting open the roasted and deskinned poblanos and scraping out the middles gently with a spoon. Fill with equal parts vegan cheese.

Whisk together the ingredients for the batter and then dip the filled poblanos carefully into the batter to coat. Roll gently into the ground pecans and then place on a silicone or parchment-covered baking sheet. Use a toothpick or two to hold them together if needed.

Bake for 25 to 30 minutes or until the cheese is melted and pecans are golden brown.

RECIPE NOTE

To roast the peppers, line a baking sheet with foil and place the peppers on the sheet. Bake at 400°F (200°C, gas mark 6) for 25 minutes or so until the skin begins to blister away from the pepper and it can be easily removed. Once softened, remove skins completely.

"CHEDDAR AND BACON" DILLED DEVILED TOFU BITES

These are a fun way to liven up a get-together and offer a variety of options for presentation. Cut them into "rustic egg shapes" as I've done in the photo, or step it up a notch and use small, basic-shaped cookie cutters (such as stars and hearts) to add a little pizzazz. A small ½-teaspoon metal measuring spoon works perfectly to scrape out the tofu to make a spot for the filling to rest.

• • • • • • • • • • • • • • • • • •   YIELD: 8 APPETIZERS   • • • • • • • • • • • • • • • • • •

1 block (14 ounces, or 397 g) extra-firm tofu, pressed for 8 hours

Black salt to taste

FOR THE FILLING:

¾ cup (180 g) cooked and drained chickpeas

1 tablespoon (6 g) nutritional yeast

2 tablespoons (22 g) yellow mustard

2 teaspoons turmeric

FOR THE TOPPING:

¼ cup (20 g) crumbled Smokey Tempeh "Bacon" recipe on page 158

¼ cup (16 g) fresh dill leaves

Smoked paprika

Cut the pressed tofu into about 8 even blocks and scoop out a cavity about ½-inch (1 cm) deep and 1-inch (2.5 cm) wide in each using a small melon baller or metal rounded measuring spoon. Sprinkle with black salt. Place the scooped-out tofu in a food processor along with the rest of the ingredients for the filling. Pulse several times until very smooth, making sure to scrape down the sides as necessary.

Transfer the filling into a piping bag fit with a large tip. Pipe into the scooped-out tofu blocks and top with bacon crumbles, dill, and paprika. Chill for 2 hours before serving.

BAKED POUTINE

Even those of us not from Canada have most likely heard of poutine.
For some, the mere description of thick-cut French fries, slathered in a rich,
salty gravy, and dotted with creamy cheese is enough to send us into
a food fantasy frenzy. But if high-caloric, animal-laden goods are
not your style, have no fear: Baked Poutine is here!

• • • • • • • • • • • • • • • •   YIELD: 4 GENEROUS SERVINGS   • • • • • • • • • • • • • • • •

FOR THE BAKED FRIES:

8 large yellow or waxy potatoes

3 tablespoons (45 ml) olive oil

2 teaspoons sea salt

Dash celery salt

FOR THE GRAVY:

¼ cup (56 g) vegan margarine

½ cup (80 g) superfine brown rice flour

3 cups (700 ml) water

3 cubes (teaspoons) beef-flavored vegetable bouillon powder

6 tablespoons (90 ml) gluten-free soy sauce

2 tablespoons (28 ml) vegan Worcestershire sauce

Few dashes liquid smoke

1 cup (112 g) vegan mozzarella-style cheese shreds, or chunks of pale vegan cheese, such as a block of Daiya Havarti flavor, cut into ½-inch (1 cm) cubes

TO MAKE THE BAKED FRIES: Preheat the oven to 400°F (200°C, gas mark 6). Cut the potatoes into thick slices so that they resemble steak fries. Toss with olive oil, sea salt, and celery salt and spread onto an ungreased, but well-seasoned, metal baking sheet.

Bake for 40 to 45 minutes, turning once halfway through, until deep golden brown on both sides and crispy.

TO MAKE THE GRAVY: Place a 2-quart (2 L) saucepan over medium heat and add the margarine and brown rice flour. Mix and cook until clumpy, about 1 minute. Whisk in the water and bouillon and continue to cook until it begins to thicken, about 5 minutes. Add the soy sauce, Worcestershire sauce, and liquid smoke and keep stirring until pretty thick, about the consistency of a smooth cake batter.

TO ASSEMBLE: Place the potatoes in a bowl and top with clumps of cheese. Pour the gravy on top and serve immediately.

AVOCADO, TOMATO, AND CHEDDAR SOUP

This slightly spicy soup is one of my favorite comfort foods.
I love to make up a big batch and freeze the leftovers in individual
freezer-safe plastic bags or plastic tubs so I always have a bowl on
hand when the craving for a piping hot bowl of creamy soup strikes.

YIELD: 6 SERVINGS

- **1 green pepper, diced**
- **1 large onion, diced**
- **1 large can (30 ounces, 840 g) canned tomatoes and juice**
- **1 tablespoon (6 g) salted vegetable broth powder (or 2 cubes bouillon)**
- **5 cups (1.2 L) water**
- **2 cloves garlic, minced**
- **1 teaspoon coriander**
- **1 teaspoon sea salt**
- **1 teaspoon paprika**
- **1 teaspoon chili powder**
- **1 teaspoon black pepper**
- **½ cup (56 g) Cheddar-style shredded vegan cheese**
- **½ cup (48 g) nutritional yeast**
- **2 avocados, peeled, pitted, and diced**
- **¼ cup (4 g) chopped cilantro leaves**

Place all the ingredients up to the vegan Cheddar cheese in a large pot and bring to a boil. Once boiling, reduce the heat just to keep it at a constant simmer and let cook for about 35 to 45 minutes or until the onions are very soft.

Add the cheese and nutritional yeast and let cook about 5 minutes or until the cheese is fully melted. Stir in the avocados and cook an additional 1 to 2 minutes. Top with cilantro right before serving.

RECIPE NOTE

Avocados are ripe when the flesh feels soft under gentle pressure from your thumb. Prevent quick browning of the flesh by simply squeezing a bit of lemon or lime juice onto it.

CHESTNUT SOUP WITH BAKED APPLE CRISPS

I love this soup more than I love the smell of late autumn and
the apples and chestnuts that accompany it. Well, that may be a stretch,
but it is quite delicious. You're more than welcome to use fresh roasted
chestnuts here (which may require a bit of extra liquid to thin),
but I recommend canned, as fresh are hard to come by but once a year.
The best brand of canned chestnuts I have found is Clement Faugier, which can
be ordered online from several vendors listed on the Grocery Guide page.

YIELD: 4 SERVINGS

FOR THE APPLE CRISPS:

1 medium-size apple, skin on, sliced very thinly

Dash sea salt

FOR THE SOUP:

1 onion, chopped

2 leeks, cleaned and sliced, tough green tops removed

1 parsnip, sliced into thin coins

1 stalk celery, minced

1 tablespoon (15 ml) olive oil

1 teaspoon sea salt

1 cup (235 ml) almond milk

1 cup (145 g) whole canned chestnuts, drained

Few leaves sage, whole

2 cups (475 ml) additional almond milk or vegetable broth to thin

TO MAKE THE CRISPS: Preheat your oven to 425°F (220°C, gas mark 7) and line a baking sheet with parchment paper. Lightly salt the apple slices and bake for 10 minutes, flipping once halfway through.

Reduce the heat to 250°F (120°C, gas mark ½) and bake until dried out, about 1 to 1½ hours, keeping an eye on them as they bake to prevent burning. Let cool.

TO MAKE THE SOUP: In a medium-size frying pan over medium-high heat, sauté the onion, leeks, parsnip, and celery along with olive oil and sea salt just until browned on the edges, about 8 minutes. Add the almond milk and simmer on medium heat until the parsnips are tender and all liquid is gone, about 20 minutes.

Transfer the sautéed vegetables along with the chestnuts and sage to a blender or food processor and blend until smooth, slowly incorporating the 2 cups (475 ml) almond milk or vegetable broth to thin. Serve hot and topped with apple crisps.

"CHEDDARY" CHEESE WHEEL

This recipe yields a soft cheese with a mild Cheddary bite, which is perfect for spreading on crackers or mixing into stews or pasta dishes. It's also delicious crumbled and baked on top of the Farinata Pizza (page 95).

• • • • • • • • • • • • • •   YIELD: 1 CHEESE WHEEL OR 12 SERVINGS   • • • • • • • • • • • • • • • •

2 cups (280 g) raw cashews, soaked overnight

½ to 1 cup (120 to 235 ml) water, to thin

1 teaspoon sea salt

1 tablespoon (15 ml) lemon juice

2 teaspoons probiotic powder

3 tablespoons (18 g) nutritional yeast

2 teaspoons turmeric

½ teaspoon vegetable broth powder

Place the cashews in a food processor and add ½ cup (120 ml) water. Blend and if more water is needed, add it, but try and keep the additions as minimal as possible, while still ensuring a smooth blend. Let the cashews blend until completely creamy, about 7 minutes. Pulse in the rest of the ingredients until combined.

Line a cereal-size bowl with cheesecloth and pour the cashew mixture into the bowl. Twist the cheesecloth to form into a round patty and tie the cheesecloth tightly with kitchen twine. Place on a wire rack, weigh down with a large heavy can, cover, and let rest 24 to 48 hours.

Bake at 170°F (77°C), or the lowest temperature your oven will go, for 2 to 3 hours. Return to the fridge and let chill before slicing.

HOAGIES

This delicious bread is used for the bun in the Philly Cheesesteak (page 182) and also for the base of the Pepperoni Rolls (page 185). The best part about this recipe is the versatility! You can place the dough into muffin tins for dinner rolls or spread flat to make focaccia. Be creative!

•••••••••••••••••• YIELD: 2 10-INCH (25.5 CM) HOAGIES ••••••••••••••••••

1½ cups (240 g) superfine brown rice flour

1 cup (136 g) sorghum flour

½ cup (96 g) potato starch

3 teaspoons (9 g) xanthan gum

1½ teaspoons baking powder

1 teaspoon sea salt

2 packets (18 g) dry active yeast

¼ cup (48 g) organic sugar

2 cups (475 ml) warm water

2 teaspoons vinegar

1 tablespoon (12 g) ground flaxseed meal mixed with ¼ cup (60 ml) water

¼ cup (60 ml) olive oil

In a large mixing bowl, sift together the brown rice flour, sorghum flour, potato starch, xanthan gum, baking powder, and salt.

In smaller bowl, dissolve the yeast in sugar and water and let sit until foamy (about 5 minutes). Add the vinegar, prepared flaxseed meal, and olive oil.

Stir the wet ingredients into the flour mix. If using an electric mixer, mix on medium high for about 2 minutes.

Using lightly oiled hands, divide the dough in half and shape into two 9-inch (23 cm) long hoagie loaves. Place on a lightly oiled baking sheet or mat. Let rise in a warm place for 50 minutes.

Preheat the oven to 375° F (190°C, gas mark 5). Bake the loaves for about 25 to 30 minutes or until golden brown on top. Let cool and then slice in half with serrated knife.

RECIPE NOTE:

These delicious Hoagies can accompany your Philly Cheesesteak. See the recipe, page 182.

PHILLY CHEESESTEAK

I'm fortunate enough to live in Philadelphia, home of the cheesesteak, where even plenty of vegan cheesesteak options exist! Although you won't find any vegan versions at the city's biggest (and best) rivals, Geno's and Pat's, which dwell across from one another in South Philly, feel free to enjoy this steak sandwich and whiz, as Pat's ordering sign advises, "wit or wit-out" onions and peppers.

• • • • • • • • • • • • YIELD: 2 LARGE CHEESESTEAKS "WIT" WHIZ AND ONIONS • • • • • • • • • • • •

FOR THE WHIZ:

3 medium yellow and orange bell peppers, sautéed

2 carrots, steamed

1 cup (96 g) nutritional yeast

½ cup (120 ml) almond milk

½ to 1 teaspoon sea salt, to taste

5 tablespoons (35 g) almond flour

½ teaspoon yellow miso

1 clove garlic

TO MAKE THE WHIZ: Combine all ingredients and whirl in a food processor until creamy, about 7 minutes. Add more almond milk if needed to thin.

FOR THE STEAK:

1 package (8 ounces, or 225 g) Butler Soy Curls

2 vegetable bouillon cubes

Very hot water (about 176°F/80°C)

½ tablespoon liquid smoke

¼ cup (60 ml) vegan Worcestershire sauce

1 tablespoon (6 g) vegetable broth seasoning

1 cup (235 ml) water

¼ cup (60 ml) gluten-free soy sauce

1 tablespoon (15 ml) olive oil

TO MAKE THE STEAK: In a medium-size bowl, place the Soy Curls, bouillon, and just enough hot water to cover. Let sit about 10 minutes until the Soy Curls are rehydrated. Drain the Soy Curls and place them back in the bowl.

Add the rest of the ingredients and combine. Let rest at least 10 minutes and then squeeze the excess liquid from the Soy Curls. Toss with about 1 tablespoon (15 ml) additional olive oil and then sauté in a large frying pan over medium-high heat until crispy, about 15 minutes, adding a touch more soy sauce for color.

FOR THE ONIONS AND PEPPERS:

1 red onion, sliced thin

1 green pepper, sliced thin

1 tablespoon (15 ml) olive oil

1 teaspoon sea salt

In a large frying pan, sauté the onion and green pepper with the oil and salt over medium-high heat for about 10 minutes and then reduce the heat to medium and let cook until caramelized, about 15 minutes.

TO ASSEMBLE THE SANDWICH: Slice a hoagie (recipe, page 181) in half lengthwise and stuff with steak, onions, and green peppers. Then top with whiz. Serve with fries and seltzer.

"PEPPERONI" ROLLS

These delicious rolls are straight from the wild, wonderful hills
of West Virginia. I used to enjoy these in the summertime when
I visited family there as a child and am happy to have them back in
my life in this animal-friendly, gluten-free version.

• • • • • • • • • • • • • • • • •   YIELD: 4 ROLLS OR 8 SERVINGS   • • • • • • • • • • • • • • • • • • •

FOR THE BREAD:

1 recipe Hoagies (see page 181)

FOR THE "PEPPERONI":

1 block (14 ounces, or 397 g) extra-firm tofu, well pressed for about 3 hours

2 cloves garlic, grated

1 large shallot, grated

3 tablespoons (48 g) tomato paste

1 teaspoon cumin seeds

1 teaspoon coriander

1 teaspoon white pepper

2 teaspoons black pepper

3 teaspoons (4 g) red chile pepper flakes

2 teaspoons fennel seeds

1 teaspoon black mustard seeds

1½ teaspoons smoked paprika

1 teaspoon sea salt

¼ cup (60 ml) + 2 tablespoons (28 ml) olive oil

¼ cup (60 ml) + 2 tablespoons (28 ml) water

1 tablespoon (20 g) red jam (e.g., lingonberry, cherry, or red raspberry)

Slice the block of tofu into about 20 small sticks. Place in a shallow dish. Combine the rest of the ingredients in a separate bowl and then pour over the tofu.

Let marinate overnight.

Preheat the oven to 300°F (150°C, gas mark 2).

Remove the tofu from the dish, reserving the marinade, and transfer to a parchment-covered baking sheet. Top with the marinade. Bake for 3 hours, flipping halfway through.

Prepare the dough for the hoagies and then lightly grease 4 miniature loaf pans. Spread about ½ cup (115 g) dough onto the bottom of each of the pans and snugly place 4 to 5 strips of pepperoni on top of the dough. Top with about ½ cup (115 g) more dough to completely cover the pepperoni. Let rest 30 minutes in a warm spot while you preheat your oven to 375°F (190°C, gas mark 5).

Bake for 30 to 35 minutes. Let cool completely before serving.

CHICKEN-FRIED TEMPEH WITH GRAVY

This finger-licking good dish is hard to resist and very much like the chicken-fried steak I ate in my pre-vegan days. Even if you're not a huge fan of tempeh (like myself), try this dish. The crunchy, crispy "skin" of this recipe will convert you immediately.

• • • • • • • • • • • • • • • • • YIELD: 4 CHICKEN-FRIED TEMPEH STEAKS • • • • • • • • • • • • • • • • •

FOR THE TEMPEH:

- **1 block tempeh (8 ounces or, 227 g), cut into 4 even "steaks"**
- **1 cup (160 g) superfine brown rice flour**
- **1 teaspoon sea salt**
- **1 teaspoon fried chicken seasoning**

FOR THE BATTER:

- **½ tablespoon ground chia seeds mixed with ¼ cup (60 ml) water**
- **½ cup (120 ml) almond milk**
- **½ teaspoon baking powder**
- **1 teaspoon sea salt**
- **1 tablespoon (8 g) gram flour**
- **Vegetable oil for frying**

FOR THE GRAVY:

- **2 tablespoons (28 g) vegan margarine, softened**
- **¼ cup (40 g) superfine brown rice flour**
- **1 tablespoon (6 g) chicken-flavored vegetable broth powder**
- **Plenty of fresh cracked black pepper**
- **1 cup (235 ml) almond milk**
- **Sea salt to taste, optional**

Rinse the tempeh briefly under running water and place onto a plate.

Whisk together the superfine brown rice flour with the sea salt and fried chicken seasoning. Set aside.

Prepare the batter by whisking all the ingredients together until smooth and allowing to rest at least 5 minutes.

Preheat your deep fryer to 365°F (182°C).

Dip the moistened tempeh patties into the flour mixture, then into the batter to coat, and once again back into the flour mixture. Immediately place into the hot oil and allow to cook for 5 minutes or until golden brown. Place the fried tempeh steaks on a paper bag or paper towel–covered tray to absorb excess oil.

Make the gravy by whisking together the margarine and superfine brown rice flour in a saucepan and cooking over medium heat until thickened, about 7 minutes. Add the rest of the ingredients and whisk continuously to prevent any lumps from forming. Keep cooking until thickened, about 5 to 7 minutes. Pour the gravy over the plated tempeh and serve while hot.

CHICAGO-STYLE DEEP DISH PIZZA

Classic Chicago-style deep-dish pizza is meant to be eaten
with a fork, and it's good to have a napkin handy!

•••••••••••••••• YIELD: 1 DEEP-DISH PIZZA (8 TO 10 SLICES) ••••••••••••••••

FOR THE CRUST:

1½ cups (240 g) superfine brown rice flour

¼ cup (48 g) potato starch

¼ cup (51 g) sweet white rice flour

1 teaspoon cream of tartar

1 tablespoon (18 g) ground psyllium husk

⅓ cup (75 ml) coconut oil or nondairy margarine, slightly softened

1¼ cups (285 ml) warm water, about 110°F (43°C)

1 packet active dry yeast (9 g)

1 tablespoon (13 g) sugar

1¼ teaspoons salt

1 tablespoon (12 g) ground chia seeds mixed with ¼ cup (60 ml) water

FOR THE SAUCE:

1 can (28 ounces, or 785 g) whole tomatoes, drained and crushed

1 can (6 ounces, or 170 g) tomato paste

3 tablespoons (39 g) sugar

1 tablespoon (4 g) minced oregano

1 teaspoon fennel seed

1 small onion, shredded and drained briefly until the extra liquid is removed

2 tablespoons (28 ml) red wine

1 heaping tablespoon (3 g) minced basil

3 cloves garlic, grated

Dash red pepper flakes (optional)

FOR THE FILLING:

2 cups (224 g) mozzarella-style shredded vegan cheese

TO MAKE THE CRUST: In a large electric mixing bowl, combine the superfine brown rice flour, potato starch, sweet white rice flour, cream of tartar, and psyllium husk until well mixed. Using a pastry blender, cut the coconut oil or margarine into the flour mixture until evenly incorporated.

In a separate, smaller bowl, mix the warm water with the yeast and the sugar and proof until foamy, about 5 minutes. Add the yeast water along with the salt and prepared chia seed to the flour mixture and mix on medium speed until well blended, about 1 to 2 minutes.

Grab a small section of dough, about the size of a golf ball, and reserve. Place the remaining dough between 2 sheets of plastic wrap and roll until thin, to about ¼ inch (6 mm). Place the smaller section of dough between 2 separate pieces of plastic wrap and roll as thin as possible.

TO MAKE THE SAUCE: Place all the sauce ingredients in a small bowl and stir together until smooth.

TO ASSEMBLE THE PIZZA: Preheat the oven to 450°F (230°C, gas mark 8). Grease an 8-inch (20 cm) springform pan with margarine and dust with finely ground cornmeal. Drape the large portion of the rolled-out dough into the pan and shape to sit evenly in the pan, about 3-inches (7.5 cm) deep. Top with cheese, then the thin section of remaining rolled-out dough.

Top with sauce and then bake for 30 minutes.

Reduce the heat to 400°F (200°C, gas mark 6) and bake an additional 30 minutes. Broil 5 minutes and let cool about 15 minutes before slicing. This pie is messy, so offer a fork when serving.

SEARED "SCALLOPS" WITH WHITE TRUFFLE SAUCE

With king oyster mushrooms available at natural foods stores or Asian groceries, there is no reason to eat another scallop ever again. The fragrant truffle oil in the sauce comes together nicely with the seared mushrooms to replicate a very haute dish found along the eastern shores of the United States.

• YIELD: 10 "SCALLOPS" • • • • • • • • • • • • • • • • • • •

FOR THE "SCALLOPS":

2 large king oyster mushrooms

½ cup (120 ml) sweet white wine, such as Riesling or Pinot Grigio

½ cup (120 ml) filtered water

3 tablespoons (42 g) vegan margarine

Sea salt

Cracked black pepper

FOR THE TRUFFLE SAUCE:

3 cloves garlic, minced

1 sweet onion, minced

Dash sea salt

1 teaspoon olive oil

1 cup (235 ml) almond milk

1 cup (235 ml) vegetable broth

¾ teaspoon additional sea salt

3 tablespoons (30 g) superfine brown rice flour

¼ to ½ teaspoon truffle oil (white or black)

TO MAKE THE "SCALLOPS": Rinse, peel, and slice the king oyster mushrooms into 1-inch (2.5 cm) thick coins. Soak the mushrooms in the white wine and water and cover. Let rest overnight, flipping over one time while marinating. The next day, squeeze the excess liquid gently from the mushrooms.

Place a medium-size frying pan over medium-high heat. Place 3 tablespoons (42 g) margarine in the pan and melt. Keep the heat at about medium to medium high and watch the margarine carefully so it does not smoke.

Sprinkle each side of the mushroom with sea salt and black pepper and then place into the hot margarine so that each is touching the pan evenly. Let cook over medium-high heat for about 7 minutes on each side, removing the pan from the heat every now and again to prevent the hot margarine from scorching. Cook until golden brown on each side and very tender.

TO MAKE THE SAUCE: Place a small saucepan over medium heat. Add the garlic, onion, salt, and olive oil and let cook over medium heat until caramelized, about 15 minutes. Add the almond milk and vegetable broth and allow the mixture to come up to medium-high heat. Do not let the sauce come to a boil. Whisk in the 3 tablespoons (30 g) superfine brown rice flour and let cook over medium heat about 5 minutes or until thickened, stirring constantly.

Once thickened, stir in the truffle oil. Arrange the "scallops" on a plate and top with truffle sauce. These are wonderful when served on a bed of lightly sautéed spinach leaves, zucchini, or asparagus spears.

TRIPLE MUSHROOM WHITE LASAGNA

Out of all the recipes in this book, I'd say that this recipe singlehandedly received the best response from all the testers and awesome friends and family whom I tossed it out to. My husband especially raved about this one, requiring me to make several pans of it during the course of writing this book.

• YIELD: 12 SERVINGS •

1 package (16 ounces, or 455 g) brown rice lasagna noodles (Tinkyada brand recommended)

FOR THE SAUCE:

1 head cauliflower, cored and cut into florets

3 cups (420 g) raw cashews, soaked for at least 3 hours and drained

1¼ cups (285 ml) almond milk

2 tablespoons (12 g) nutritional yeast

1½ teaspoons sea salt

1 tablespoon (15 ml) lemon juice

FOR THE FILLING:

2 cups (140 g) each shiitake mushroom caps, whole crimini, and oyster mushrooms, sliced

1 tablespoon (1.7 g) minced fresh rosemary

2 cloves garlic, minced

1 cup (160 g) minced shallots (about 9 small)

Sea salt

1 tablespoon (15 ml) olive oil

2 cups (224 g) mozzarella-style shredded vegan cheese

Preheat the oven to 375°F (190°C, gas mark 5).

Cook the lasagna noodles according to package directions (if using Tinkyada brand, cook only 15 minutes). Once cooked, rinse gently with cool water and place on parchment-covered baking sheets arranged in a single layer. Mist gently with olive oil and cover with another piece of parchment.

At the same time the noodles are cooking, steam the cauliflower by placing it in a steamer basket over a large stockpot containing about 2 inches (5 cm) of water. Bring the water to a boil and cover. Let cook about 5 to 7 minutes or until fork tender. Remove from heat.

Place the steamed cauliflower, soaked cashews, almond milk, nutritional yeast, sea salt, and lemon juice in a food processor and let blend until very smooth, about 7 to 9 minutes. You many need to do this in batches depending on the size of your food processor.

In a large frying pan, sauté the mushrooms, rosemary, garlic, shallots, sea salt, and olive oil over medium-high heat for about 12 minutes or until most of the liquid has been cooked out of the mushrooms and they begin to caramelize around the edges.

Lightly grease a 9 x 13-inch (23 x 33 cm) baking dish and line the bottom with 3 noodles. Top with about 1 cup (225 g) sauce and then sprinkle with filling. Top with about ⅓ cup (37 g) vegan cheese. Repeat with 3 more layers, ending with sauce and cheese.

Bake for 50 minutes, covering with foil for the first half of cooking. Once cooked through and the cheese is melted, broil for 5 minutes to give the top a toasted glow.

CHICK'N STRIPS IN PEANUT MOLE

Mole sauce is so popular and so varied in Mexico, it is often referred to as Mexico's curry. The sauce, which features bittersweet chocolate and chiles, is among my favorite flavors in Mexican cuisine.

• YIELD: 6 SERVINGS •

FOR THE CHICK'N STRIPS:

- 1 package (8 ounces, or 225 g) Butler Soy Curls
- 4 cups (950 ml) very hot water
- 2 chick'n vegetable bouillon cubes or 2 teaspoons chick'n vegetable bouillon
- 1 tablespoon (15 ml) olive oil for frying

FOR THE MOLE SAUCE:

- 1 tomato
- 4 cloves garlic
- 2 to 4 Mexican green chile peppers
- 1 serrano pepper
- 1 tomatillo, quartered
- 4 ounces (115 g) bittersweet chocolate (70 percenet cocoa), melted
- 1 teaspoon cinnamon
- ½ teaspoon cloves
- 2 cups (230 g) corn Chex-type cereal (make sure it's gluten-free) or gluten-free bread crumbs
- 3 cups (700 ml) salted vegetable broth

TO MAKE THE CHICK'N STRIPS: Place the Soy Curls into very hot water along with the vegetable boullion. Let rest 10 minutes and then drain well. Squeeze any excess liquid from the Soy Curls and then toss into a large, deep-sided, nonstick frying pan along with about 1 tablespoon (15 ml) olive oil. Sauté the Soy Curls over medium-high heat, until lightly browned and crispy, about 10 minutes. Stir often and make sure you have a well-oiled pan, as Soy Curls tend to stick. Remove from the heat and set aside.

TO MAKE THE MOLE SAUCE: Preheat your oven to broil. Place the tomato, garlic, and pepper on a foil-covered baking sheet. There is no need to remove the seeds or stem from the tomato or peppers. Let cook about 45 minutes or until blackened, turning occasionally to cook evenly and keeping a fairly close eye on them. The tomato will not be as blackened as the peppers, but it will turn very soft and wrinkly when ready. The peppers will be blackened on all sides, and the garlic should simply be fragrant and softened.

Once all are roasted, rinse the peppers and tomato under cold water to gently remove the skins and stems. Let cool completely and then place in a blender along with the tomatillos, melted chocolate, cinnamon, cloves, Chex cereal, and broth. Blend until smooth, about 2 minutes.

TO FINISH: Place the sauce over the prepared Soy Curls in a large, deep-sided frying pan and bring to a boil over high heat, stirring often so as not to burn the sauce. Immediately reduce the heat to medium and let simmer, covered, for about 15 minutes, stirring occasionally. The sauce will thicken slightly upon heating.

Serve over rice, in a burrito, or as a main addition to a taco buffet.

ALMOND-CRUSTED TOFU WITH BLACKBERRY SAUCE

This crispy, crunchy tofu dish reminds me of popcorn chicken, and the bite-size morsels pair well with the sweetness and tartness of the sauce. These freeze well if you'd like to make up a few batches and then bake them when desired. Just preheat your oven to 400°F (200°C, gas mark 6) and bake the frozen tofu puffs for 5 to 10 minutes or until hot throughout and crispy on the outside.

YIELD: 6 SERVINGS

FOR THE TOFU:

- 1 package (14 ounces, or 397 g) extra-firm tofu, drained and pressed at least 3 hours
- ¼ cup (30 g) gram flour
- ¼ cup (60 ml) water
- ½ teaspoon sea salt
- 1½ cups (168 g) almond meal

FOR THE SAUCE:

- 1 cup (145 g) fresh or frozen blackberries
- 2 tablespoons (28 ml) full-bodied red wine, such as Bordeaux
- 2 tablespoons (26 g) granulated sugar
- Dash sea salt
- 1 tablespoon (8 g) cornstarch
- 2 tablespoons (28 g) very cold water

TO MAKE THE TOFU: The day before making, place the drained and pressed tofu in a freezer-safe plastic bag and seal tightly. Freeze overnight and then let thaw on the countertop a few hours until no longer frozen through. Slice the tofu carefully into equal-size squares.

Preheat the oven to 400°F (200°C, gas mark 6).

In a small bowl, whisk together the gram flour, water, and salt. Make sure no lumps remain.

Place the almond meal in a separate bowl.

Dip each square of tofu first into the flour mixture, allowing any excess to drip. Coat evenly. Next, dip into the almond meal to coat and place on a baking sheet lined with a silicon mat or parchment paper.

Bake for 20 minutes, flip, lightly salt, and then bake about 15 more minutes until the tofu is browned on all sides.

TO MAKE THE SAUCE: To make the sauce, combine all ingredients through the sea salt in a small saucepan and heat up over medium heat, stirring occasionally, for about 8 minutes, or until the berries begin to break apart.

Mix together the cornstarch with cold water until very smooth and then stir into the blackberries. Turn off the burner and let thicken and cool, about 10 minutes. Serve the crispy tofu with the sauce either drizzled on it or on the side for dipping.

MAPLE PUMPKIN PIE WITH CINNAMON WALNUT CRUST

The Canadian province of Quebec produces almost three-quarters of the world's maple syrup on production farms called sugarbushes. The delicious sap is transformed into syrup by boiling it to the point where it has just the right sugar content. From there it is enjoyed over pancakes or waffles and used extensively in baking, such as in pumpkin pie, a favorite in Canada. This pie encapsulates both maple syrup's unique flavor and distinct sweetness that complements the pumpkin beautifully.

•••••••••••••••• YIELD: 1 STANDARD-SIZE PIE (8 SERVINGS) ••••••••••••••••

FOR THE CRUST:

2 cups (200 g) walnuts, ground

¼ cup (60 g) packed brown sugar

1 cup (160 g) superfine brown rice flour

1 teaspoon cinnamon

¼ cup (56 g) vegan margarine

1 tablespoon (12 g) ground chia seeds

¼ cup (60 ml) cold water

FOR THE FILLING:

½ cup (120 g) brown sugar

½ cup (160 ml) maple syrup

1 teaspoon ground cinnamon

1 teaspoon fresh grated ginger

½ teaspoon ground cloves

¾ teaspoon salt

½ cup (120 g) silken tofu

¼ cup (40 g) superfine brown rice flour

1½ cups (368 g) pumpkin purée, from a can

½ cup (120 ml) coconut milk

⅓ cup (40 g) finely crushed walnuts, for topping

Preheat the oven to 400°F (200°C, gas mark 6).

Combine all the ingredients for the crust in a food processor for about 2 minutes or just until crumbly, scraping down the sides as necessary. Remove and press into the bottom of an ungreased pie pan (the bottom of a glass works well here). Poke holes in the crust with a fork and bake for 10 minutes. Remove from the oven.

Increase the oven temperature to 425°F (220°C, gas mark 7). Purée all the "filling" ingredients in a food processor or blender until very smooth. Spread evenly into the prebaked crust.

Bake the pie for 13 minutes; reduce the heat to 350°F (180°C, gas mark 4) and bake for 45 to 50 minutes more. Let cool completely, top with crushed walnuts, and then transfer to the refrigerator. Chill overnight before cutting.

WHITE CHOCOLATE RASPBERRY CHEESECAKE WITH DARK CHOCOLATE CRUST

I could go on and on about my love for cheesecake, but if I had to pick just one variety of cheesecake to enjoy, this would be it. Even though vegan white chocolate is difficult to source in stores, it is easily available online from various retailers, many times not marked as vegan at all. Just look for a variety that doesn't contain any milk, milk fat, or butterfat, or make your own from scratch, and you're good to go!

•   YIELD: 16 SERVINGS   •

FOR THE TOPPING:

1 cup (125 g) raspberries

½ cup (100 g) sugar

1 teaspoon vanilla

2 teaspoons cornstarch whisked with ¼ cup (60 ml) water

FOR THE CRUST:

2 cups (240 g) walnuts or pecans, ground

¼ cup (24 g) plus 1 tablespoon (6 g) dark cocoa powder

¼ cup (50 g) sugar

½ teaspoon sea salt

1 tablespoon (12 g) ground chia seeds mixed with ¼ cup (60 ml) water

FOR THE FILLING:

3 tubs (8 ounces, or 225 g each) vegan cream cheese

¼ cup (50 g) sugar

1¾ cups (300 g) vegan white chocolate, chips or chunks, melted

1 block (11 ounces, or 325 g) silken tofu, drained

7 tablespoons (70 g) superfine brown rice flour

¼ cup (60 ml) lemon juice

1 teaspoon vanilla extract

TO MAKE THE TOPPING: Place a small saucepan over medium heat and add the raspberries, sugar, and vanilla. Cook for about 2 minutes, while mashing gently with a fork or potato masher. Drizzle in the cornstarch slurry and stir until thickened. Remove from the heat.

TO MAKE THE CRUST: Preheat the oven to 400°F (200°C, gas mark 6).

In a medium-size bowl, combine all the ingredients for the crust. Transfer to an 8-inch (20 cm) springform pan and press down across the bottom of the pan. Poke holes in the crust using a fork. Bake for 15 minutes. Remove from the oven and let cool.

TO MAKE THE FILLING: Increase the oven temperature to 425°F (220°C, gas mark 7). Blend all the ingredients for the filling in a food processor until very smooth, about 7 minutes, or until absolutely no lumps remain.

Spread the filling evenly over the crust. Bake for 10 minutes. Leave the cake in the oven and reduce the oven temperature to 250°F (120°C, gas mark ½).

Let cook 45 minutes without disturbing. Remove from the oven, cover with sauce (or leave it separate for serving), and let cool 2 hours at room temperature and then overnight in the refrigerator before attempting to cut.

GROCERY GUIDE

Gluten-Free:
The Gluten-Free Mall
866-575-3720
www.celiac.com/glutenfreemall/

Free from Gluten
877-745-8836
www.freefromgluten.com/

Whole Foods Market
512-477-4455
http://wholefoodsmarket.com/

Wegmans
800-WEGMANS
www.wegmans.com/

Trader Joe's:
www.traderjoes.com/

Food for All Market
www.foodforallmarket.com/

Gluten-Free Shop
011 61 3 9578 6400

Vegan:
Food Fight Grocery
503-233-3910
http://foodfightgrocery.com/

Vegan Essentials
866-88-VEGAN
www.veganessentials.com/

Indian:
Desimart
800-IS-DESIMART
www.desimart.com/

iShopIndian.com
877-786-8876
www.ishopindian.com/

Mexican:
MexGrocer.com
877-463-9476
www.mexgrocer.com

Cool Chile Co.
011 44 870 902 1145
www.coolchile.co.uk/

Middle Eastern:
Dayna's Market
313-999-1980
www.daynasmarket.com/

Shamra
301-942-9726
www.shamra.com

Asian:
Asian Food Grocer
888-482-2742
www.asianfoodgrocer.com/

Wing Yip Store
0121 327 6618
www.wingyipstore.co.uk/

African:
African Hut
949-582-9546
www.africanhut.com/

Satooz
011 61 7 3353 9939
www.satooz.com/

ACKNOWLEDGMENTS

To every single person in the world who had or has ever taught someone how to prepare a meal; all the input of individual influences and personal translations of each recipe from one generation to the next, one continent to the other, have created the vivid and lively global feast that we all enjoy today.

To Sally Ekus and Lisa Ekus and the rest of the gang at the amazing agency The Lisa Ekus Group (Sean, Corinne, Jaimee, and everyone else). You guys all know how much I adore working with you, but I'll say it again: I'm so happy to be represented by your team. Thank you so much for everything.

To Amanda Waddell and Cara Connors for being such amazing editors. Thank you both for all of your hard work and thoughtful input. And a big thank you to all the others at Fair Winds Press, including Betsy Gammons, who made this book come to life!

To Landen, for being a great big brother and a fantastic helper throughout my writing and recipe development—especially with your little delightful sister, Olive. Olive, thank you for being so sweet.

To JD for always being there for me to lean on, both literally and figuratively.

To my steadfast and wonderful testers Lisa Pitman, Jenni Mischel, Jim Allen, Dianne Wenz, Jen Pitoniak, Melissa Schneider, Megan Clarke, Mokina Soria Caruso, and Kristina Sloggett. Thank you all for helping with these recipes, and ultimately with the first round of edits to the recipes. I appreciate you and all your help more than I could ever say.

To Laurel VanBlarcum for being a wonderful friend and a lovely set of eyes to look over my work. It's such a pleasure to have gotten to know you over the years. Thank you.

To all my lovely readers of my books and my blog. Thank you so much for being there. You all are the main reason I adore my job.

To all my wonderful friends who talk to me daily, weekly, monthly, or even yearly. I adore you. Thank you so much for being there.

To all the fantastic people in Philadelphia, both new friends and old, who have welcomed me into the community with warm and open arms. You truly do know how to make a girl feel at home in the City of Brotherly Love.

INDEX